The MOB Lynching of Frank Fisher

Mike Robinette

Published by Mike Robinette, 2022.

THE MOB LYNCHING OF FRANK FISHER

First edition. April 30, 2022.

ISBN: 979-8201380823

Written by Mike Robinette.

Table of Contents

Acknowledgments

First, I want to thank my awesome wife, Rhonda. From reading drafts to giving me advice on topics and most of all for holding down the fort so I could travel to do research and do writing for hours on end at home. She was as important to this book getting done as I was. Thank you so much, dear.

Galion History Center
Tanesha Pickering
Galion Public Library
Crawford County Recorder
Crawford County Engineer
Public Library of Mount Vernon and Knox County
Fredericktown Community Library
Cincinnati & Hamilton County Public Library
Columbus Metropolitan Library
Cleveland Public Library
Dayton Metro Library
Greene County Library
State Library of Ohio
Ohio History Connection
University Libraries – Bowling Green State University
Miami University Libraries
Robin Bash
Sharon Dockstader
Joy Hansen

Preface

While growing as a teenager in Galion, Ohio in the 1960s, I heard the story I am sure was heard by most that lived there; "the last black person that lived in this town was hanged".

I always wondered if this story was a nasty rumor or the nasty truth. Living in Galion, you couldn't help but notice there were no blacks in our neighborhoods or schools. In fact the minority population currently remains very small in Galion (97% white). Some 50 years after first hearing the story of the "lynching, I decided to do a search for the truth. Sadly and not surprisingly I found the "nasty rumor" was indeed the "nasty truth".

My first verification of the truth came from a search of newspaper archives. After a few searches, there it was, staring me in the face, the cold dark truth from a May 2, 1882 article in the Cincinnati Enquirer.

The seven headlines from that one article were as follows;

MOB LAW.
Its Terrible Execution at Galion.
The Lynching of Frank Fisher in the Broad Light of Day.
For the Fiendish Crime Committed Upon Little Barbara Rettig.
Deaf in the Entreaties of the Mayor and Other Officers in Desist.
The Unmasked, Determined Mob Marches the Monster to His Death.
Recognized by His Victim – A Day of Intense Excitement – How the Work Was Finished.

I decided to keep digging and the more I did the worse the nightmare became. Not only was there a Black American hung in Galion in 1882, it was obvious the execution of Frank Fisher happened with the support of community leaders of Galion. Perhaps not surprising, for the time, the print media feed the flames of hate and outrage. The more I read about this public murder the more I felt the full story (as much as could be discovered) needed to be told.

Introduction

"While I do not justify lynching, I know of no other punishment which is adequate to suppress the crime for which lynching is usually resorted to." Bishop William Montgomery Brown (SEE Appendix D)

Much of what happened that gruesome weekend in the spring of 1882, will never be known. The people involved only survive through stories told by family members of subsequent generations and the minimal records that still exist. Most of the story comes from newspaper articles that are conflicting in many details. The only reporting, other than newspapers and a brief mention or listing in a few books or reports, comes from Dr. Bernard "Doc" Mansfield who by all accounts was the leader of efforts to preserve Galion's history for over 50 years of his life. Doc Mansfield led the effort to create the Galion Historical Society (now Galion History Center) in 1955. Doc Mansfield died May 11, 2012 and was a 1940 graduate of Galion High School. He wrote and compiled the first history of Galion, "The Olentangy Legacy", two volumes, published in 2010. Doc Mansfield includes some never reported information regarding the lynching in book two, pages 37-50.

My efforts involved digging deeper into the story of Frank Fisher's lynching, including Frank Fisher's background (although very limited information is available) and the many others involved in his murder. For the first time the various newspaper coverage of the Lynching will be analyzed and compiled. In addition research into the background of the various participants is included. Lastly maps and pictures of the locations and facilities involved with Frank Fisher's lynching are provided.

In telling the story of the Lynching of Frank Fisher it is important to have at least an overview of the early history of the environment for Black Americans in Ohio, Crawford County and Galion. This examination is included in Part One. Part Two details the research regarding the lynching of Frank Fisher from the alleged rape, to his hunt and capture, his lynching and burial and the aftermath and investigation.

The following short book details the results of my search for the truth; as much as I could be discover. There is one truth, however, that needs no further research. Frank Fisher was murdered by a Galion mob on Sunday, April 30, 1882.

When quoting sources, I use the words "Colored and "Negro" as used in the source material even though those words today are considered inappropriate.

Part One

Black Americans in 19th Century Ohio

To better understand what lead to the lynching of Frank Fisher it is helpful to have a broad understanding of the political and social climate that existed for Black Americans in the early years of Ohio's history.

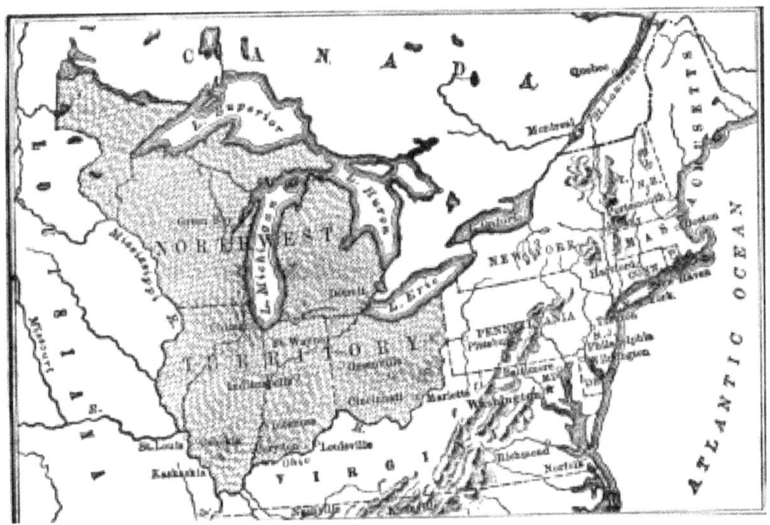

Figure 1 Map of Northwest Territory

Ohio's history begins with the Ordinance of 1787, better known as the Northwest Ordinance. In many ways, the Northwest Ordinance can be viewed Ohio's first "constitution." It not only established a government for the Northwest Territory - a prerequisite for the orderly settlement of the west - but also set the terms for the admission of Ohio and four other states into the union.

Figure 2 Map of Ohio and Counties 1802

The prohibition against slavery as well as other individual rights contained in the Northwest Ordinance's Articles of Compact were to remain "forever remain unalterable." This effort to bind the states, however, became the subject of an intense legal and political debate especially concerning the continuing legal effect of the Northwest Ordinance's prohibition against slavery. The fundamental rights protected by the Northwest Ordinance, including the prohibition against slavery, became part of the 1802 Ohio Constitution and remain to this day part of the Ohio Constitution.

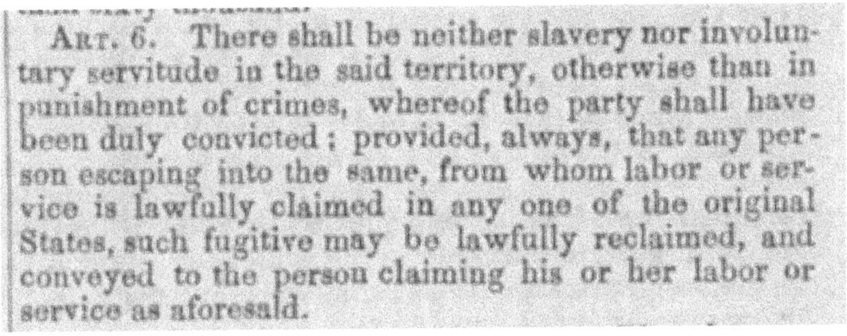

ART. 6. There shall be neither slavery nor involuntary servitude in the said territory, otherwise than in punishment of crimes, whereof the party shall have been duly convicted; provided, always, that any person escaping into the same, from whom labor or service is lawfully claimed in any one of the original States, such fugitive may be lawfully reclaimed, and conveyed to the person claiming his or her labor or service as aforesaid.

Figure 3 Northwest Ordinance wording regarding slavery

A study of the free Black Americans in Ohio during the first half of the nineteenth century makes clear one basic fact. The free Black American was a member of a servile race and was never a welcome inhabitant of the state. He was an orphan of society, unwanted and ignored. Events during the first fifty years of Ohio's existence as a state show an increasing opposition to the settlement of Black Americans under any circumstances. The North as a whole rejected slavery, but also seemed to reject embracing the free Black American. Much of the basis for opposition to the free Black American was brutally practical. The Black American seemed ignorant, shiftless, and irresponsible and in point of fact he generally was—a system of forced labor does not foster in a man qualities of stability, ambition, and frugality. Slavery does not prepare a man for the industriousness necessary to overcome other man-made barriers such as prejudice and misunderstanding. Simply stated, in Ohio prior to the Civil War, although there was never any significant proslavery sentiment, there was wide-spread discrimination and second-class treatment given the free Black American which grew in proportion to the amount of Black American influx. [1]

1802 Ohio Constitutional Convention

In April, 1802, Congress enacted legislation authorizing the residents of the Ohio Territory "to form for themselves a constitution and state government" as a step toward being "admitted into the Union upon the same footing with the original states, in all respects whatever."

The vote on the Act followed party lines, with the Republicans (Jeffersonian) favoring rapid creation of states from the Northwest Territory and the Federalists steadfastly rejecting such a course. The Ohio Enabling Act provided for the election on October 12, 1802, of delegates for a constitutional convention. The thirty-five delegates who were elected convened in Chillicothe on November 1, 1802.

Some of the most contested issues at the convention involved the status of Black Americans. The delegates never voted on a proposal to introduce slavery - at least not on the floor of the convention. There were, however, two votes on the slavery issue recorded in the convention's journal, but they involved votes on involuntary servitude and indentures.

Although there seems to have been no serious support for a pro- slavery amendment at the convention, opposition to slavery did not translate into support for Black American rights. On November 22, 1802, the committee of the whole submitted a draft that limited suffrage to white male residents who paid or were charged with a state or County tax. The convention defeated by a vote of 19 to 14 a motion to omit the word "white" from that section.

> A motion was then made, further to amend the said article at the Secretary's table, by striking out, after the word "all," in the first line of the first section, the word "white."
>
> And on the question thereupon, it passed in the negative—yeas 14, nays 19.

Figure 4 - Record of first vote to grant Ohio's Black Americans the right of suffrage

Whatever the practice within the various states, only one eighteenth-century state constitution, the South Carolina Constitution of 1790, imposed an express racial qualification for voting. Thus, Ohio was only the second state, and the first non-slave state, to give constitutional sanction to racial discrimination in voting qualifications. Ohio's decision to impose a racial qualification for voting is particularly noteworthy when considered in the light of the suffrage requirements outlined in the congressional Act of 1802 that authorized the calling of a constitutional convention in Ohio. That Act, while imposing taxpayer, gender, and residency requirements for those voting to select convention delegates, never mentioned race. One is thus led to the conclusion that the Ohio Constitution may have disenfranchised some voters who had previously been eligible to vote in Ohio. The Ohio Constitution's banishment of Black Americans from the ranks of the politically relevant citizenry was not limited to voting.

Following an unsuccessful motion that would have eliminated the tax requirement on voting, a motion to enfranchise "all male negroes and mulattoes now residing in this territory . . . if they shall within months make a record of their citizenship" passed by a vote of 19 to 15.

Another motion was then made further to amend the said section, by adding to the end of the section a proviso, in the words following:

Provided, That all male negroes and mulattoes, now residing in this territory, shall be entitled to the right of suffrage, if they shall within months make a record of their citizenship.

And on the question thereupon, it was resolved in the affirmative—yeas 19, nays 15.

Figure 5 - Record of the second vote on granting right of suffrage to Ohio's Black Americans

This victory for Black American suffrage, however, was short-lived. Four days after extending the franchise to Black Americans, the convention reconsidered the issue and voted 17 to 17 on a motion to strike the entire amendment. The tie required Edward Tiffin, the President of the convention, to cast the deciding vote, and he joined his fellow Virginia Republicans, including the leaders of the Chillicothe faction, in opposing suffrage. Though he had freed his own slaves, Tiffin believed that "the immediate neighborhood of two slave-holding States made it impolitic to offer such an inducement for the influx of an undesirable class to the new State."

A motion was made to amend the said article, by striking out after the word "election," in the seventh line of the first section, the words following: " Provided, That all male negroes and mulattoes now residing in this territory, shall, at the age of twenty-one years, be entitled to the right of suffrage, if they shall, within one year, make a record of their citizenship with the clerk of the county in which they may reside; and, provided also, that they have paid or are charged with a state or county tax."

And on the question thereupon, it was resolved in the affirmative—yeas 17, nays 17.

The Convention being equally divided, and Mr. President declaring himself with the yeas.

Figure 6 - Final vote rejecting suffrage to Ohio's Black Americans

Following the initial votes on Black American suffrage, the delegates voted 19 to 16 to approve an anti-civil rights amendment that denied "negroes and mulattos" the right to hold office, serve in the military, and testify in any court against a white person. Tiffin voted with the majority to deny Black Americans these specific rights - the only time he voted other than to break a tie. On November 26, the same day Tiffin broke the tie and denied Black Americans suffrage, the convention reconsidered its earlier vote and defeated the anti-civil rights amendment by a single vote. In effect, the convention decided to let the legislature determine the rights of Black Americans.

Rather than split the convention, the Black Americans in Ohio were not assumed to be parties to the Constitution. At the outset, then, Black Americans in Ohio were legally free but achieved little else during the next half century. The unsympathetic attitude of the Convention members toward the free Black American was to be the dominant attitude for some decades.

Ohio, carved from the Northwest Territory, which by the provisions of the Northwest Ordinance could be called "the valley of democracy," was the most stringent of all the Northern states with anti-negro legislation. Less than two years later, the legislature would begin passing laws limiting negro rights.

Ohio's Black Laws

The Black Laws, plus the state's constitution, serve to point out Ohio's official attitude toward free Black Americans: prohibit slavery, keep the Black American out, degrade Black Americans in the state, and allow slavery to continue outside Ohio.

As early as 1804, during the second session of the Legislature, attention was called to the increasing immigration of "colored" people into the State. This ingress of "free negroes" was looked upon by many as a great calamity. From the beginning the Southern counties had received a large proportion of their settlers from Kentucky and Virginia, and by them the free blacks were always regarded as despicable and entitled neither to the respect nor charity of the whites.

There was also another contingent who, while not Southern themselves, were so bound to them by social and business relations that they could always be relied upon by the South for sympathy and support. The influence of these two classes was great enough to secure in the Legislature a bill which should tend to restrict Black American immigration, in reality, a fugitive slave bill. This feature, no doubt, was in response to complaints from Kentucky and Virginia planters that their slaves were escaping into Ohio and were there aided by Ohio citizens to make their escape into Canada. This bill declared that no Black American should be allowed to settle in the State unless he could furnish certificates from some court in the United States of his actual freedom. The same law also enjoined that all Black Americans who were already residents in the State should register before the first of the following June, with the names of their children, in the records of the County clerk. The fee for registering was 12 1/2 cents per name.

Still further to increase the heavy burden of the "colored" immigrant, it was made a penal offense to employ a "negro" for one hour unless he could present a certificate of freedom, and any violator of this law should be fined not less than $10 nor more than $50.

The same penalty was attached to the humane act of harboring or hindering the capture of a fugitive slave, and for aiding his escape from the State the same should be fined $1,000; the informer thereof usually received one-half the fine, thus placing a premium on spying and tale-bearing, and there were never wanting unscrupulous men ready to testify against anyone who might employ a Black American, for the sake of the reward. Besides his fine the would-be friend of the fugitive slave must pay to his owner 50 cents per day for his service.

These are the main provisions of the Act of 1804, the first statute respecting the Black American enacted by the Legislature of Ohio, and laid the foundation for the notorious "Black Laws." The same spirit which inspired the Act of 1804 inspired nearly every other act on the subject from that time until 1849.

In 1807, to more effectually discourage Black American immigration, the law of 1804 was so amended that (a) no Black American should be allowed to settle in Ohio unless he could within twenty days give bonds to the amount of $500 signed by two bondsmen, who should guarantee his good behavior and support. (b) The fine for harboring or concealing a fugitive was raised from $50 to $100, one-half to go to the informer and one half to the overseer of the poor in the district. (c) The proposition made in the constitutional convention (1802), to prohibit Black American evidence against a white person, was revived, and it became a statute law of the State of Ohio that no Black American should be allowed to give evidence in any case where a white man was a party. This law caused incalculable mischief to the Black Americans. It put them at the mercy of unscrupulous white men. A white man could rob, beat and kill a "colored" man, and unless some white person was present he could escape all punishment. A case is recorded where a white man escaped conviction of murder where there were eight "colored" eye witnesses, simply because sufficient testimony of white men could not be found.

After the passage of the law of 1807, the political status of the Black American remained substantially the same for the next forty-two years. "Colored" immigration was discouraged as much as possible, and yet every year an increasing number of free "Black Americans

", or emancipated slaves from the South, crossed the Ohio River, hoping to find a home in a Free State. They came to find that the law required a certificate of freedom and a bond guaranteeing their good behavior and support before they were even allowed to settle in the State. From all this we see that if the Black American settler was maltreated, robbed or injured in any way by his white neighbor, there was no redress open to him. If he would avenge his wrongs he must do it by retaliation, and return the offense in its own kind. He found the courts closed to him if a white man however great a scoundrel, was the aggressor. If white blood flowed in his veins a man could outrage a Black American to his "heart's content" and be perfectly safe from punishment, if a Black American was the only available witness against him.

By a law passed as early as 1824, and again in 1828 and 1831, black men were excluded from ever serving as jurymen. Even the privilege of shouldering his musket in defense of his white neighbor's country was denied the "colored" patriot, for the militia as well as the jury was closed to anyone who had more Black than Caucasian blood. If he would redress his wrongs at the polls, he found the ballot, too, was not his to use. His property could be taxed, his own status fixed by an assembly which he had no voice in electing; no matter how light his complexion, and many times it was fairer than the white voter's ; the ballot was refused him if he was even suspected of being a black man.

It is very clear that the Black American in Ohio possessed only a quasi-legal position; in fact, it was explicitly stated in a law passed 1829, providing for the maintenance of the "poor," that nothing in the act should be so construed as to permit a black or mulatto person to gain a legal settlement in the State.

The repeal of the "Black Laws" was finally passed, February 10, 1849.

From this time there was a marked change in the sentiment of the people regarding the Black American. As soon as they were given a legal standing in the courts they were treated more as men. There was, however, but little disposition to grant them suffrage, and still less to treat them as social equals, and admittance to the public schools was still denied, yet very many privileges and rights as citizens were extended to them. By the same act, repealing the "Black Laws," separate schools for "colored" children were established. Thus the free "colored" man at home shared in the general sympathy which began to be expressed for his less fortunate brothers in bondage. The tide of public prejudice, which had so long deprived him and his children of the rights and protection of law, was now slowly receding, and Ohio was beginning to rank as a strong anti-slavery State.

1850 Ohio Constitutional Convention

From the first day of the Ohio constitutional convention convened in Columbus, May 6, 1850, the question of the status of the Black American in the State was prominent in the deliberations of the convention. The greatest diversity of opinion existed among its members; some were willing to allow him every legal privilege accorded the white man, some would deprive him of those already possessed, while others would drive him from the State altogether, and forever bar the doors against Black American immigration.

As early as the third day of the convention, a memorial was presented from the citizens of Lorain and Hardin counties, praying the convention to authorize the State Legislature to pass an act for the extradition of "colored" people in the State. Petitions asking for extradition or for laws prohibiting "colored" immigration continued to pour in upon the convention. As many as three were received in one day. Those petitioners who desired prohibition of immigration generally asked that the law denying to Black Americans the right of testifying in a case where whites were party, be revived and embodied in the Constitution, or in the statute laws of the State. Proposals for State aid to colonization were sometimes coupled with these petitions. These petitions reveal the extreme anti-Black American sentiments held by many in the State. This feeling, as has been said before, was strongest in the southern counties bordering on the Ohio river, as the population here, was largely from the South, who from birth and education, or from social and business relations, were heartily in sympathy with their old home interests and institutions, and most naturally cherished a strong antipathy for the Black American, whether free or slave, who found a home in Ohio.

The views of former President Andrew Jackson also influenced the debate on elections and suffrage. The Jacksonian principle of popular democracy led to a general agreement on the need to provide for the election of judges and other government officials and on the elimination of the tax requirement on voting. While universal manhood suffrage for whites passed without debate, the delegates bitterly debated the status of Black Americans. Slavery was not at issue, but suffrage and equal rights for Black Americans aroused some of the strongest feelings at the convention. Some delegates even objected to the receipt of petitions supporting Black American rights, especially petitions from Black Americans themselves.

William Sawyer of Auglaize County, the most outspoken opponent of civil and political rights for Black Americans, found such petitions "revolting" and refused to "permit even his fellow citizens to petition that Black Americans shall be entitled to all of the privileges and immunities of white men, without raising his voice against it. Sawyer believed that blacks were an inferior race, that slavery had benefited blacks, and that the principle espoused in the Declaration of Independence that all men were created equal only applied to the Anglo Saxon race. He also predicted "bloodshed" and "persecution" if Black Americans were permitted to vote. Another delegate, Simeon Nash of Gallia County, argued that given the public sentiment the delegates risked having the constitution defeated by the voters if they proposed a constitutional amendment allowing Black Americans to vote.

Sawyer's extreme views may not have been shared by a majority of delegates, but there is no question that there was strong anti-black sentiment at the convention and in many parts of the state. In fact, the convention received petitions not only in opposition to suffrage and equal rights for blacks but also in support of both a ban on black immigration into Ohio and for funds for colonization of blacks to create, in effect, an "Ohio in Africa." James Worthington, a delegate and the son of Thomas Worthington, agreed with the observation that "at the time of the Revolution there was less prejudice against the black race than there is at present" and in the future it was likely that "the longer the two races occupy the same soil, the greater will be their revulsion and the stronger the prejudice.

The vote to remove the word "white" from the section on voter qualifications failed by a vote of 66 to 12.

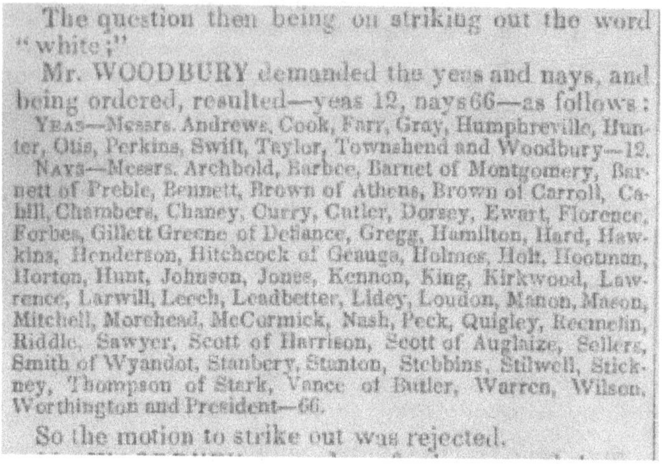

The question then being on striking out the word "white;"

Mr. WOODBURY demanded the yeas and nays, and being ordered, resulted—yeas 12, nays 66—as follows:

YEAS—Messrs. Andrews, Cook, Farr, Gray, Humphreville, Hunter, Otis, Perkins, Swift, Taylor, Townshend and Woodbury—12.

NAYS—Messrs. Archbold, Barbee, Barnet of Montgomery, Barnett of Preble, Bennett, Brown of Athens, Brown of Carroll, Cahill, Chambers, Chaney, Curry, Cutler, Dorsey, Ewart, Florence, Forbes, Gillett Greene of Defiance, Gregg, Hamilton, Hard, Hawkins, Henderson, Hitchcock of Geauga, Holmes, Holt, Hootman, Horton, Hunt, Johnson, Jones, Kennon, King, Kirkwood, Lawrence, Larwill, Leech, Leadbetter, Lidey, Loudon, Manon, Mason, Mitchell, Morehead, McCormick, Nash, Peck, Quigley, Reemelin, Riddle, Sawyer, Scott of Harrison, Scott of Auglaize, Sellers, Smith of Wyandot, Stanbery, Stanton, Stebbins, Stilwell, Stickney, Thompson of Stark, Vance of Butler, Warren, Wilson, Worthington and President—66.

So the motion to strike out was rejected.

Figure 7 - William Cahill, the representative from Crawford County was one of 66 nay votes.

Following this vote, James Taylor of Erie County moved to amend the section by allowing the legislature "to extend the right of suffrage to inhabitants of this State not hereby qualified as electors." Taylor's amendment was defeated 68 to 11. Thus, the convention ensured not only that suffrage would be limited to whites but that the legislature could do nothing about it. Black Americans, however, would be counted for the purpose of apportionment. William Cahill of Crawford County voted Nay

The delegates also rejected a motion to remove the word "white" from the article on the militia by a vote of 66 to 22. The state militia would consist only of white males.

The question then being on striking out the words "all white male citizens, residents," for the purpose of inserting the words "all male citizens;"

Mr. HOLMES demanded the yeas and nays, which were ordered, and resulted—yeas 22, nays 62—as follows:

YEAS—Messrs. Andrews, Barbee, Brown of Athens, Clark, Cook, Ewing, Farr, Gray, Greene of Defiance, Hitchcock of Cuyahoga, Humphreville, Hunter, Larsh, Mason, Orton, Otis, Perkins, Sawyer, Swift, Taylor, Townshend and Woodbury—22.

NAYS—Messrs. Barnet of Montgomery, Bennett, Blickensderfer, Brown of Carroll, Cahill, Case of Hocking, Chambers, Collings, Curry, Dorsey, Florence, Forbes, Gillott, Graham, Green of Ross, Gregg, Groesbeck, Hamilton, Hard, Harlan, Hawkins, Henderson, Hitchcock of Geauga, Holmes, Hootman, Horton, Hunt, Johnson, Jones, Kennon, Kirkwood, Larwill, Leadbetter, Lidey, Loudon, Mason, Mitchell, Morehead, Morris, McCloud, Nash, Patterson, Peck, Quigley, Reemelin, Riddle, Roll, Scott of Auglaize, Scott of Harrison, Smith of Highland, Smith of Warren, Stanbery, Stilwell, Stickney, Stidger, Struble, Swan, Thompson of Shelby, Thompson of Stark, Way, Worthington and President—62.

So the motion to strike out was disagreed to.

Figure 8 - William Cahill, the representative from Crawford County was one of 62 nay votes.

The delegates rejected the amendments to ban immigration and to support the colonization of Black Americans, although these amendments received more votes than the amendment for Black American suffrage. As with suffrage, immigration and colonization generated heated debates. The amendment to ban immigration met with so much opposition, including from opponents of Black American rights who pointed out that such a ban had been tried under the Black Laws for forty years and failed and would likely violate the U.S. Constitution, that it was withdrawn. In its place, proponents of the anti-immigration policy moved to add a section allowing the legislature to discourage the immigration of blacks "consistent with the Constitution of the United States." This motion failed by a vote of 58 to 39.

Mr. Cahill representing Crawford County was not present for this vote.

The commonly told history of antebellum race relations in the Midwest, especially in Ohio, is one of a bleak and dismal landscape, with discrimination everywhere. [2]

The complex story of race and rights in Ohio is vital to our understanding of race relations in mid-nineteenth century America. Ohio reflected the changing, complex nature of race relations throughout the North, as well as changing attitudes toward slavery. In the early part of the century, Ohio was hostile to slavery within its own boundaries, but most Ohioans were relatively unconcerned about the existence of the institution in other states. Early Ohio was antipathetic to the presence of African Americans and discouraged them from moving into the state; however, it simultaneously provided tough punishments for people kidnapping free blacks.

The best study of post-civil war race relations in Ohio summarized the antebellum period with the glum conclusion, "[t]he late 1850s found most Ohio blacks pariahs, restricted and scorned, living in the state but in no accurate sense citizens." [3]

Slavery Amendments to U. S. Constitution

The 13th, 14th, and 15th Amendments to the Constitution, sometimes known as the Reconstruction Amendments, were critical to providing Black Americans with the rights and protections of citizenship. The 13th Amendment formally abolished slavery. The 14th Amendment established Black Americans as equal citizens of the United States. This amendment overturned the 1857 *Dred Scott v. Sanford* case in which Supreme Court Chief Justice Roger B. Taney had written that Black Americans were not citizens and thus had "no rights which the white man was bound to respect." Finally, the 15th Amendment gave Black American men the right to vote.

While the end of the war brought freedom to the slaves, it did not immediately improve the status of the free "colored" people in Ohio. The Thirteenth Amendment, abolishing slavery, was, of course, ratified by the Ohio Legislature, without opposition. The action of the General Assembly respecting the Fourteenth Amendment is somewhat curious. Congress proposed this amendment to the States in June, 1866, and in January, 1867, the Assembly in Ohio passed a resolution of ratification. But in just one year and three days from that time, the Assembly passed a resolution rescinding their former resolution of ratification. In the midst of this controversy over the Fourteenth Amendment, on April 6, 1867, the Assembly resolved to submit to the people an amendment to the State Constitution granting the right of suffrage to all male citizens of above twenty-one years of age. This action anticipated the proposal of the Fifteenth Amendment by nearly two years, and its results determined the vote of the General Assembly when that amendment was submitted to it. The people of Ohio, even after the four years' war which secured the emancipation of the slaves, were yet in no humor to grant their own free Black Americans the right of suffrage.

The proposed amendment to the State Constitution as offered April 6, 1867, was defeated at the October elections, 1867, by the large majority of 50,000. This vote shows very plainly that a large part of the citizens of Ohio had no disposition to acknowledge the Black American as a political equal, and entitled to the rights and privileges of the white man.

Crawford County voted against suffrage for Black Americans by a vote of 3,788 no and 1,703 yes. Polk Township including Galion voted against 582 to 312.

Two years before this proposed Constitutional amendment, the Ohio Democratic State Convention, which assembled in Columbus August 24, 1865, declared "that the effort now being made to confer the right of suffrage upon Black Americans was an invidious attempt to overthrow popular institutions, by bringing the right to vote into disgrace!" And further declared that if allowed to vote, the Black Americans would hold the balance of power in State politics, and white demagogues and renegades, by pandering to the Black American, would secure control of the State government; and still further, that the white laborer, by Black American competition, would soon be reduced to the condition of the Russian serf and "Ohio would become the Black American paradise and the white man's wilderness."

In order to render more effective the will of the people, the Legislature, April 16, 1868, passed an "Act to Preserve the Purity of Elections." The object of this law was to minimize as much as possible the "Black American's" chances for casting a vote. The provisions were very elaborate and numerous. Any person offering to vote, with the slightest visible admixture of Black blood, was compelled to take a solemn oath to truthfully answer the questions put to him. Then followed a long list of questions, whose object was to elicit a confession that he was a Black American, and if any person secured the right to vote by false swearing, he was adjudged guilty of perjury and a sentence of from three to ten years in the penitentiary followed, while the judge of elections who received the vote of a Black American was liable to six months' imprisonment in the County jail, and a civil action might be brought against him to the amount of $500 by any elector in the County where such vote was cast.

The Act to Preserve the Purity of Elections passed the Ohio Senate by a vote of 20 yeas' and 12 nays', State Senator C. Berry Jr. of Upper Sandusky, the senator representing Seneca, Crawford and Wyandot counties, voted yea.

The Act passed the Ohio House by a vote of 55 yeas' and 45 nays', the Ohio House of Representative from Crawford County George M. Ziegler of Galion voted yea.

Such was the law and sentiment of Ohio respecting Black American suffrage when Congress submitted to the Legislature the Fifteenth Amendment, which prohibited the States from denying or abridging the right of suffrage "on account of race, color or previous condition of servitude." The spirit of this amendment was entirely contrary to the policy pursued by the State from its formation. In Constitutional and statute laws the people had repeatedly declared against Black American suffrage, and only the year before they had given a decided expression of preference not to amend the then existing laws of the State.

The Fifteenth Amendment was proposed by Congress, February 6, 1869, and immediately sent to the States for their ratification, and on May 4, the Ohio Legislature forwarded to Congress a solution refusing to ratify the amendment, on the grounds that Ohio had, only two years before, by a large majority, "rejected negro suffrage."

Regarding the above, State Senator Berry representing Crawford County, among others, voted yea on H.J.R No. 147.4. State Representative James Robinson also voted yea.

Though this action of the General Assembly was not wholly unexpected, yet it caused such a degree of excitement, and such a significant pressure was brought to bear upon the members of that body, that it convinced them that a reconsideration of their resolution would not be unacceptable to the people. Moreover, it was plainly evident that the amendment was going to secure ratification by a sufficient number of States to insure it's becoming a law, regardless of the action of Ohio. Consequently the Legislature wisely decided to reconsider, and a motion for ratification was carried in both houses, with only a meager majority in the Senate. The joint resolution was forwarded to Congress on January 27, 1870.

The vote on S. J. R. 4 ratifying the proposed 15th amendment passed on the Ohio Senate by a vote of 19 yeas and 18 nays. State Senator Alexander E. Jenner, representing Crawford, Seneca and Wyandot counties voted nay. The ratification vote passed in the Ohio House of Representatives by a vote of 57 yeas and 55 nays. Representative James Robinson of Crawford County voted nay.

Two months later it had received the ratification of the necessary number of States, and March 30 it was declared in force. Universal male suffrage was henceforth the fixed policy of the United States. Ohio's reluctant ratification of the amendment had attracted the attention of the whole country, and when she decided to follow the course which her sister States, some by inclination, others by necessity, had adopted, a resolution from both houses of our National Council was forwarded to Governor Hayes, congratulating "the Legislature of the noble State of Ohio in her ratification of the crowning measure of reconstruction" It is to be hoped that our Government will never have cause to repent the course they then adopted, and that the Black Americans in Ohio will never make themselves unworthy of the political privileges then extended them. The passage of this amendment ended the long struggle for political equality. Hence forth the Black American in Ohio was to be legally the equal in every respect of his white fellows.

Environment for Black Americans in 19th Century Crawford County and Galion

Figure 9 - Ohio Map of Counties, Galion Represented by Red Circle

The Democratic Party controlled the politics by significant majorities in the 19th century history of Crawford County and Galion. Along with this political affiliation came strong anti-Black American attitudes.

"Crawford County since the time of Andrew Jackson has been a Democratic County, and since the County courthouse was built in 1856, with one exception no republican ever held County office, and that one republican was not elected but got there by appointment." [4]

In the elections for Governor between 1885 through 1899 Ohio elected 4 democrat and 19 republican governors. In those same years Crawford County voted for the democratic candidate in every election by substantial majorities. The lowest percentage (53.13% majority) going to the democratic candidate in

1855 and the highest percentage (69.02%) going to the democratic candidate in 1873. Even the Democrats controversial and loosing candidate Vallandigham carried the county with 57.75% of the vote.

Crawford County voted for the democratic candidate for President in every election until 1924. In the 1924 election Crawford County cast a 40.83% plurality for Calvin Coolidge, Democrat John Davis collected 30.36% and Progressive Robert La Follette received 28.67%

The elected delegate from Crawford County to the 1850 Ohio Constitutional Convention was William Cahill. Cahill was a democrat and former state representative. He voted against suffrage for Black Americans even though he was supportive of receiving petitions regarding the issue.

> Mr. CAHILL would vote on all occasions against the extension of the right of suffrage to the negro population, but was in favor of the reception of all respectful petitions.

Figure 10 - Record of Cahill Comment Regarding Black Suffrage Petition

"At the election in 1860 Crawford's vote for president was Douglas, northern democrat 2,752; Lincoln, republican, 2,064; Breckenridge, southern democrat, 117. There was no question where Crawford stood. The war broke out, and democrats and republicans alike responded to their country's call, and for a year there was a united sentiment in the County, for the defense of the union." [5]

However, this united sentiment was short lived. The Copperhead movement during the Civil War was very active in Crawford County and Crawford County became an "anti-war" county. Crawford County cast a majority of its votes for national, state and county Democratic candidates in every election held during the war and contributed its share of leaders to the movement as well as to the draft riots and the protest violence.

"Shrewd men in the rising young republican party, saw that in a successful and popular war their lease of power would be perpetuated; equally shrewd men in the democratic party, feared the disintegration of their once powerful party, and as a result first criticized, then opposed, and finally became openly hostile to the Lincoln administration and in many cases strong sympathizers with the southern cause. This feeling was mostly confined to the party leaders, for during the entire war, except among the most bitter, enlistments continued regardless of party. But it is true that the 117 Breckenridge men (voters) eventually molded the opinion of the County, and Crawford became an anti-war County.

Many altercations arose between the soldiers returning on furlough and the rougher elements in the Democratic Party and fights and knock-downs were frequent; a political meeting was almost invariably followed by assaults on citizens. In many cases shots were fired, the most serious being the result of an altercation in the Fulton drug store in Bucyrus when three soldiers were wounded, one very seriously. In many places in the country churches were desecrated, their windows broken, and two were destroyed because the minister was a union sympathizer. In the country (rural areas) also known union sympathizers found their stock poisoned, their barns and outhouses burned, and their families ostracized. It is a singular fact that when a nation is engaged in a prolonged war the baser instincts pervade human nature, and among the more ignorant and brutal the animal instincts prevail, and it was this class that led the outrages in defiance of law and of decency. The seed sown by local leaders started a force which got beyond their control. When the draft came armed resistance was prepared for, but wiser counsels prevailed and the drafts passed off quietly." [6]

"Crawford County (and Galion) had a very strong German population, and nine-tenths of them belonged to the Democratic Party, and yet a very large majority of these same German democrats were for the preservation of the Union. The majority of the people in Crawford County were loyal during the war, but the County did gain an unenviable notoriety through a disorderly element in nearly every section being allowed to commit their outrages with very little protest from their neighbors and much less restraint by the authorities. It was a case where the people controlled, not the whole people, but the worst element as in the days of the French Revolution. It not only gave the County a bad name, but it did more than anything else to bring on the intense party bitterness which it took years to overcome.

Some churches in the County were so intense in their unionism that the Christianity of a democrat was so doubted that he was compelled to sever his connection with the church, or left it voluntarily to avoid the suspicions with which he was viewed by his democratic neighbors. Other churches were composed exclusively of democrats. There were republican stores and democratic stores, republican and democratic hotels and barber shops, and nine-tenths of the trade of each came from their own partisans. So intense was the feeling that it is doubtful if a democratic store in the town had a republican clerk, and when some of the leading republican stores later had a democratic clerk they were regarded as unfaithful to their party obligations. In many churches it took careful handling by the ministers to avoid friction in their congregations." [7]

The Democratic viewpoint was enthusiastically presented by the Bucyrus Crawford County Forum, founded in 1859 by Archibald McGregor, who later became editor of the Stark County *Democrat* and the subject of a famous arbitrary war-time arrest case in 1862. Thomas Beer, who bought the Forum from McGregor in April 1860, continued its Democratic heritage and was himself elected to the Ohio House of Representatives in 1863 and 1865. During the war when the news of a Southern victory reached Bucyrus, a United States flag would appear above the newspaper's office. When word was received of a Union victory, however, the Stars and Stripes were replaced with a dove holding an olive branch in its beak, sewn upon a field of white.

In the first 120 years of existence of the State of Ohio, the Black American population grew at a rate twice the population of White Americans (reaching 6.5% of the population in 1950). The Black American population in Crawford County grew gradually since the county was established in 1840 but never exceeded 1%.

The representatives of Crawford County consistently voted against any effort to grant the rights of citizenship to Black Americans

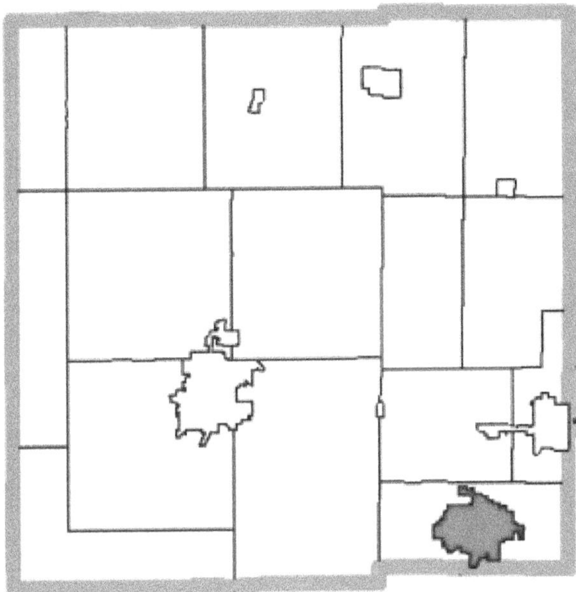

Figure 11 - Crawford County Map with City of Galion Outlined in RED

In 1840 Galion became a borough and elected Joel Todd as the first mayor. At that time Galion had a population of only 200 people. A line of stages passed through the city, and there was two taverns, three stores and several small shops, and the enterprising citizens decided they were large enough to become a village.

The city grew rapidly and in 1860 reached a population of 1,966 people and by 1870 it nearly doubled its population to 3,523, passing Bucyrus and becoming the largest place in the County, a position it held for 40 years.

After 1870 its growth continued, and by 1878 the citizens decided that they had the 5,000 people necessary to incorporate as a city. A census was taken, showing more than the requisite number, and the city of Galion was incorporated, divided into four wards. In 1879 James A. Homer was elected the first mayor; he was followed by Abraham Underwood in 1881.

Until in 1920s, the Democratic Party controlled the elective offices in Galion including Mayor, Council, Clerk, Solicitor, Treasurer and Marshal. Occasionally a republican was elected to Council from the fourth ward. The same was true of Polk Township.

Just as in the case of Crawford County, Galion's population of Black Americans grew gradually and at a lower proportion that existed in the state. In fact in 1870 through 1890 the percentage of Black Americans living in Galion exceeded the percentage of Crawford County, if however slightly.

The trend of growth in the Black population of Galion reversed starting in 1890 and dropped to less than .1% in 1920. (Appendix A)

Since the lynching of Frank Fisher the population of Black Americans in Galion has been virtually nonexistent.

What is Lynching?

A lynching is the public killing of an individual who has not received any due process. These executions were often carried out by lawless mobs, though police officers did participate, under the pretext of justice. Lynching typically evoke images of Black men and women hanging from trees, but they involved other extreme brutality, such as torture, mutilation, decapitation, and desecration. Some victims were burned alive. A typical lynching involved a criminal accusation, an arrest, and the assembly of a mob, followed by seizure, physical torment, and murder of the victim. Lynchings were often public spectacles attended by the white community in celebration of white supremacy. Photos of lynchings were often sold as souvenir postcards.

During the period between the Civil War and World War II, thousands of Black Americans were lynched in the United States. Lynchings were violent and public acts of torture that traumatized Black Americans throughout the country and were largely tolerated by state and federal officials. These lynchings peaked between 1880 and 1940 and claimed the lives of Black American men, women, and children who were forced to endure the fear, humiliation, and barbarity of this widespread phenomenon unaided.

Lynching in the United States was the widespread occurrence of extrajudicial killings beginning in the 1830s Pre-Civil War South until the civil rights movement in the 1950s and 1960s. Although the victims of lynching in the U.S. for the first few decades of the phenomenon were predominantly white Southerners, after the American Civil War emancipated roughly four million enslaved Black Americans they became the primary targets of lynchings beginning in the Reconstruction era. The American South saw the majority of lynchings as it contained the largest number of Black Americans residing there, although racially motivated lynchings occurred in the Midwest and border-states as well.

These coincided with the Great Migration of Black Americans out of the American South, and were often perpetrated to enforce white supremacy and intimidate ethnic minorities through racial terrorism. A significant number of lynching victims were accused of murder or attempted murder. Rape, attempted rape or other forms of sexual assault were the second most common accusation; often being pretexts for lynching Black Americans who violated Jim Crow era etiquette or engaged in economic competition with whites. According to Arthur F. Raper, approximately one-third of the victims were falsely accused. According to the Tuskegee Institute, 4,743 people were lynched between 1882 and 1968 in the United States, including 3,446 Black Americans and 1,297 whites.

Many historians believe the true number is underreported.

Part Two

27

The Alleged Rape

On Friday, April 28, 1882, at around noon, Barbara Rettig, who had celebrated her thirteenth birthday just two weeks earlier, was sent on an errand by her father. News reports suggest the errand was either to obtain some oats for planting, collect some wood chips for use in the stove or she was simply visiting a neighbor. One report even claims she was using a wheel barrel to collect the items of her errand.

Accordingly, Barbara headed south to the end of Market Street, which from her house was about a third of a mile and then turned left, heading east, along the Morrow-Crawford County Line Road. If Barbara was not out to "collect wood chips", how far along County Line Road it was to her appointed destination is unknown.

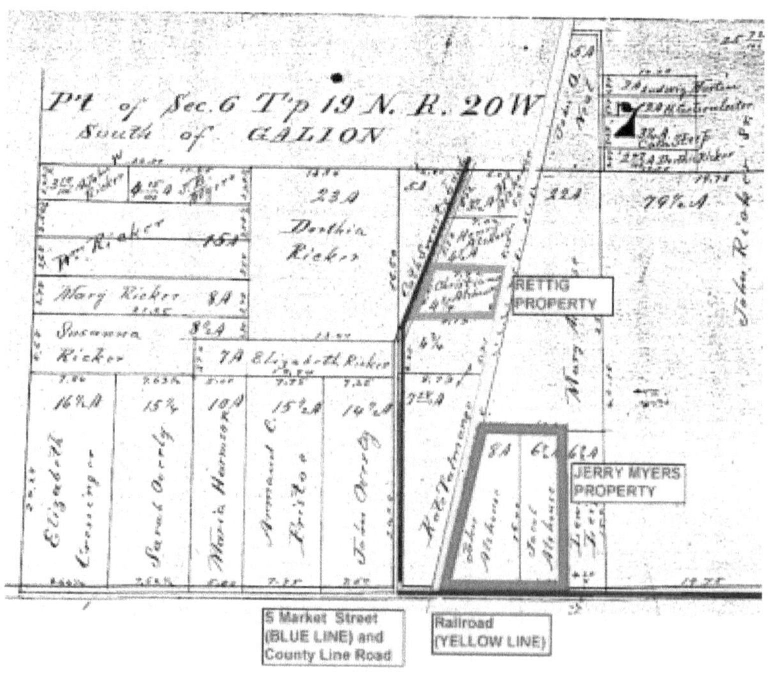

Figure 12- Map of Polk Township south of Galion 1880

Barbara found herself passing the area of the newly acquired property of Jeremiah (Jerry Myers). Myers had just the previous year purchased six and one half acres of land on March 28, 1881 (Vol 52, Page 168), from Jacob and Sarah Alshouse, for $505 and the abutting eight acres of land on June 8, 1881 (Vol 50, Page 16), from John and Hannah Alshouse, for $505. The property was located along the east boundary of the Cleveland Columbus & Cincinnati Railroad and fronted on County Line Road. It was at the site of this property where Barbara crossed the path of Frank Fisher.

Reportedly Fisher was hired by Jerry Myers to chop wood on the newly acquired property. Some news reports called the property a farm. It seems unlikely Myers was a "farmer". Myers was then over 60 years old, had worked as a railroad engineer his entire life, and lived on Union Street in Galion with his wife Sarah Jane (Long) Myers, whom he married on March 18, 1841 in Knox County, Ohio. He died January 21, 1895 and is buried at Fairview Cemetery.

It was reported, that as Barbara walked along County Line Road in front of the Myers property, she was approached by Frank Fisher "the negro wood-chopper". Fisher approached Barbara and advised her to "make no outcry or he would kill her". Fisher quickly covered her mouth with a handkerchief, bound her wrists and pulled her over the fence. Fisher then "brutally and repeatedly outraged" her for an hour, then left her unconscious.

Frank Fisher was a Black American born about 1851 in Kentucky. It has been reported that he had family in Louisville Kentucky and possibly a father and sisters in Columbus, Ohio, although neither have been verified.

According to the 1880 census of Columbus, Franklin County, Ohio Fisher was 29 years old, was born in Kentucky as was both of his parents. He worked "attending livery stable". Living at the address of the stables of Mrs. George Kirk (widowed).

The Kirk livery was located across from the state capitol building.

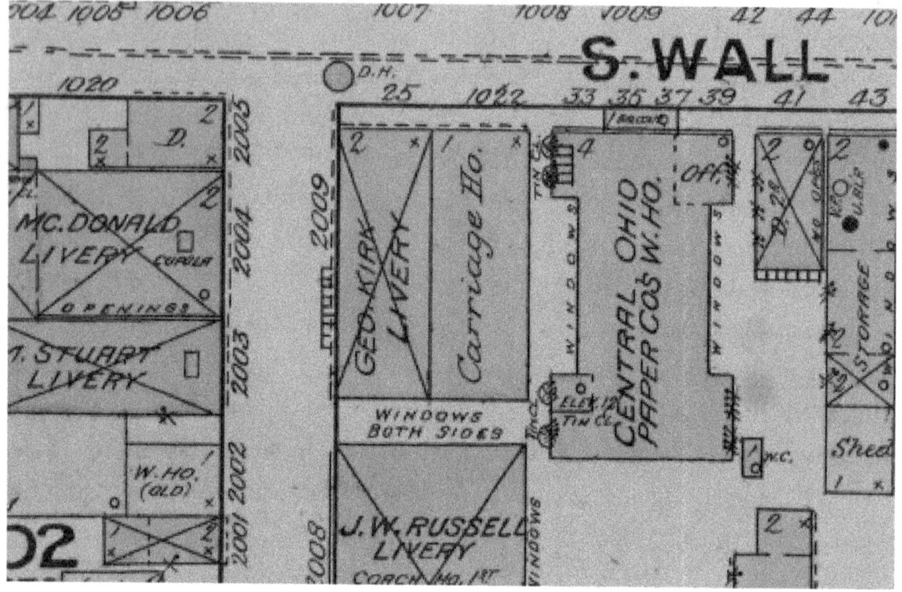

Figure 13 - Sanborn Map of Downtown Columbus 1887

The Cincinnati Commercial newspaper reported on May 2, 1882 that Fisher up until July, 1881, was last employed in Columbus at the McDonald's livery stable, at the rear of the Neil House.

The same Cincinnati Commercial article stated "he is said to have relatives here" (Columbus). The article also stated he left Columbus in "July last" (1881). The article concludes with the statement, "Those who knew him here say that he was a pretty tough customer, and it is thought that he richly deserved a hemp matinee".

The Bucyrus Telegraph Forum reported in a May 5, 1882 article that Fisher, "had a father and sisters living in Louisville, Ky."

Fisher is described in various news reports to be "a young full-blooded negro, stoutly built, slightly bow-legged, with stubby beard and not by any means a brutal appearing face. He had been working in the vicinity of Galion for some time and was considered so far as people had cared to form an opinion of him as an industrious harmless fellow."

THE MOB LYNCHING OF FRANK FISHER

The Cincinnati Enquirer reported, "Fisher, the rapist, is a very black negro, with woolly mustache and goatee, and is about five feet six inches in height."

The Galion Inquirer stated. "The ravisher was a negro of small stature, vicious appearance, badly bowed legs, and always bore a questionable character."

How and exactly when Frank Fisher arrived in Galion, Ohio is unknown. An extensive search for information on his family was unsuccessful.

Barbara Rettig was born in Germany on April 14, 1869. Her father, Peter Rettig, born September 26, 1842 and mother Anna Eva Boehm, born December 18, 1843 were also born in Germany.

Peter Rettig and Anna Eva Boehm were married November 26, 1864 in Darmstadt, Germany. Barbara had twelve siblings, six sisters and six brothers.

Barbara Rettig's family (along with her then 9 siblings) immigrated to the United States arriving on May 24, 1881. The Rettig's arrived in New York City from Bremen, Germany aboard the Habsburg. Peter Rettig listed his occupation as "tailor".

The Rettig's must have made prior plans for their arrival in Galion, Ohio, Peter Rettig purchased for $665 a 4 ¼ acre parcel of property on June 16, 1881 (Vol 48, Page 391) from a Jeremiah (Jerry) Myers and his wife. The property was located just south of the Galion City limits in Polk Township on South Market Street. This is the same Jerry Myers as the one who owned the woods where the alleged rape occurred.

Jeremiah Myers previously purchased the 4 ¼ acres on March 5, 1881 (Vol 54, Page 3), just a few months before selling the property to Rettig's, from Augustus and Christina Persky for $575. (Note this deed was not recorded until April 24, 1884)

The estate of Peter Rettig sold the 4 ¼ acres property at auction on March 27, 1926 (Vol 132, Page 229), to Clement L Wisler for $2,275 (deeded to Wisler on April 3, 1926). Wisler over the next few years subdivided and sold the property. The property now encompasses the addresses of 941 through 947 South Market Street.

Information on the early years of the Rettig family's settlement in Galion, Ohio are sketchy because the 1890 census records do not exist and other recorded information is limited.

There was a Polk Township school located at the northwest corner of South Street and Morrow-Crawford County Line Road. The school was District No. 2 and was also known as Klopfenstein. The school was closed in 1883 so it is likely if any of the Rettig children attended school before 1883 it was at District No. 2. In 1889 the Polk Township Board of Education ordered the dismantling of District No. 2 since it was closed.

The various newspapers reports all seemed to fan the flames of "outrage" concerning the alleged rape and several reported conflicting details:

The *Bucyrus Telegraph Forum* reported:

"Barbara Rettig is the daughter of a respected German citizen, residing about a mile and a half south of Galion near the Morrow County line. She is but thirteen years of age just budding into womanhood and possessed of many of the innocent graces which receive the admiration and respect of men, but arouse the base passions of creatures who disgrace the image of manhood. Her father is an employee at the New York Pennsylvania and Ohio railroad shops and, on Friday afternoon last, in obedience to his request." [8]

The *Bucyrus Telegraph Forum* reported further:

"A physician was summoned and the alarm given. Within an hour the whole city was aroused and the search for the criminal was joined by hundreds of horrified but determined men. Although no one witnessed the outrage, Fisher, fully realizing the extent of his crime and urged by a premonition of the fate in store for him if captured, fled at once and for nearly two days evaded the searchers. The pursuers scattered north south and west but for some unexplainable reason neglected the east in which direction subsequent developments showed that the fugitive had gone." [9]

The *Marion Star* gave an early report stating:

THE MOB LYNCHING OF FRANK FISHER

"The particulars of the rape case which occurred here yesterday as near as can be learned are as follows: Frank Fisher, a "colored" man was engaged to cut wood for Jerry Myers, an engineer on the Bee Line in a small piece of woods near Galion. Myers told a German family living near, when Highwarden was cutting wood they could have the chips if they would pick them up. A *little eleven year old* girl yesterday afternoon *while picking up some chips* was attacked by the brute and horribly outraged. The little girl started for home, but fell exhausted before reaching there, in which condition she was found. The brute escaped but several parties are hotly pursuing him and hope to soon overtake him." [10]

An early report from the *Cincinnati Enquirer* explained:

"A negro named Frank Fisher committed a rape upon a thirteen-year-old German girl named Barbara Rettig just south of town at noon today, repeatedly ravishing his victim for one hour, and leaving her unconscious. After recovering consciousness the girl managed to drag herself home, and told her terrible experience to her distracted parents, who at once gave alarm." [11]

In a later article the *Cincinnati Enquirer* declared:

"This has been the most exciting day in the history of this city and County. Frank Fisher, the negro who so horribly outraged the little German girl, Barbara Retting, aged only thirteen years, in the woods where he had been chopping wood, last Friday noon." [12]

The first report from the *Galion Enquirer* provided the following details:

"Last Friday afternoon about two o'clock a horrible outrage was perpetrated two miles south of this city. About that time Barbara, the thirteen year-old daughter of Peter Rettig, an employee of the N.Y.P. & O. Company, was sent to a neighbor's some distance away to *procure some oats for sowing*. She was returning on the road which separates Crawford from Morrow County, when she was approached near the Myers farm by a wood-chopper, a negro named Frank Fisher, who had been long in the employ of Mr. Myers. He told her to make no outcry or he would kill her. Quickly throwing a handkerchief over her mouth, he bound her wrists pulled her over the fence, and accomplished his hellish purpose. He then fled, no doubt being fully aware of his fate if apprehended. The poor, unfortunate creature of his brutal lust had swooned and lay unconscious for some time, but, upon return of consciousness, started for home. She had not proceeded far until she swooned again, and after many struggles reached her home, some distance from the scene of the outrage, when she was seized with convulsions, and her life despaired of. Miss Rettig is a modest little German girl of irreproachable character, and she has not rallied from the effects of the crime. The ravisher was a negro of small stature, vicious appearance, badly bowed legs, and always bore a questionable character." [13]

The *Bucyrus Journal* gave the following account of the alleged rape:

"Last Friday, 28th April, about noon, a "colored" man, known as Frank Fisher, chopping wood on the farm of Mr. Myers, on the south line of the County, and about a mile from Galion, tied a handkerchief over the mouth of a German girl named Barbara Rettig, abused her for an hour and fled.

The poor little child half-dead, frequently fainting by the way, and dreadfully distressed, tottered home told the outrage and the name of the wretch who had perpetrated it." [14]

The *Cleveland Plain Dealer* reported:

"Last Friday as Barbara Rettig, a German girl, thirteen years of age, was returning home from a neighbor's house she was assaulted by Frank Fisher, a burly negro, dragged into the woods, repeatedly and brutally outraged and left in an insensible condition. When she returned to consciousness and dragged herself home and told her story there was intense excitement and searching parties were immediately organized to look for the black beast and capture him if possible." [15]

The *Ohio State Journal* reported the same day as the alleged rape:

"A little girl named Rettig, aged thirteen, living two miles south miles south of here, was sent to a neighbor's some distance away to procure some oats for sowing. She was returning, when she was approached by a wood chopper, a negro, who told her, on the peril of her life, to make no outcry, and quickly throwing a handkerchief over her mouth dragged her to the earth, bound her wrists, pulled her over a fence and outraged her. Her condition is dangerous. The perpetrator is Frank Fisher, a negro of small stature, vicious appearance and badly bow-legged. Up to a late hour this evening he had not been caught." [16]

The *Columbus Dispatch* reported the following details:

"Miss Barbara Redick (German) aged thirteen, who was outraged in a beastly manner yesterday by Frank Fisher ("colored") is lying in a dangerous condition, and it is only by the best care that she can recover. She left her home at noon to visit a neighbor and passed by the woods where the "colored" scoundrel spied her and caught her and threw her down. She lost consciousness and two or three hours passed before she recovered. When he left he dropped some of his clothes, he has gone to parts unknown." [17]

Two days later the *Columbus Dispatch* added the following details:

"Yesterday the greatest excitement that ever occurred in our city was caused by the lynching of Frank Fisher, "colored", for the horrible ravishing of Miss Barbara Rettig, a German girl of much respectability, aged only thirteen.

Last Friday she left her father's home on an errand for parents to some of the near neighbors, and, while she was passing through the woods where the "colored" scoundrel was chopping wood for Jerry Myers, she was followed by Fisher, overtaken and thrown down. The brute stuffed something in her mouth to prevent her calling help, and abused her in an indescribable manner. The poor girl became unconscious owing to the intense pain and excitement, and remained in that state for hours." [18]

The Cleveland Leader reports Ms. Rettig is not expected to recover:

"A horrible outrage was committed here today about 12 o'clock by a negro American named Frank Fisher, his victim being a young German girl aged 13 years, daughter of Peter Rettig, who lives just outside the southern corporation limits. The child was going about a half mile from home on an errand. In passing a strip of woodland the negro approached her, and, before she was aware of his intentions, he seized her, tying a handkerchief over her mouth, threatened to kill her if she made any outcry. Leading her into the woods he repeatedly ravished her, and left her in an unconscious condition. Regaining consciousness she walked to her home in an exhausted and almost dying condition. Medical aid was at once called, but serious doubts are entertained as to her recovery. People are looking for the scoundrel in all directions, an, if apprehended there is strong talk of lynching him. Fisher is about five and one-half feet tall and wears a woolly mustache and goatee." [19]

The Cleveland Leader follows up with more detail of the alleged rape:

"This place is in a terrible state of excitement tonight over the lynching of the black fiend Frank Fisher, who committed the brutal outrage upon Barbara Rettig, daughter of Pater Rettig, a German living just south of this city, on Friday last. The victim of his lust is a mere child thirteen years old.

She had been sent to a neighbor's about half a mile distant, on an errand. In passing a strip of wood, the negro approached her, and, before she was aware of his intentions, he seized her, tying a handkerchief over her mouth, and threatened to kill her if she made any outcry. Leading her into the woods he repeatedly ravished her and left her in an unconscious condition. Regaining consciousness, she walked to her home in an exhausted and almost dying condition, and is still lying in a critical state. She was able to give a pretty accurate description of the villain, and the aroused people initiated the most vigorous search for him, recognizing from her account that the brutal perpetrator of the outrage was Frank Fisher, a burly negro." [20]

In *The Olentangy Legacy* the name of the attending physician to Ms. Rettig is named:

"Returning home, she was examined in a short while by Dr. Stiefel who discovered the cause of her collapse. Remaining at her bedside, he determined the name of her assailant." [21]

A follow up report indicates Barbara Fisher was recovering better than originally expected.

"Although having suffered great agony, mentally and physically, is rapidly recovering, and, with proper care, will be convalescent in a short time. She has received the best of care, and Mr. Rettig and family appreciate the many acts of kindness and attention bestowed upon the unfortunate child by neighbors and citizens." [22]

The Hunt

How it was decided that Frank Fisher was the guilty party in the alleged rape of Barbara Rettig is not entirely clear. What is clear is Frank Fisher was within hours a hunted man. This, even though the reports of Barbara Rettig's condition indicate she was near death, somehow enough information was gathered that pointed to Frank Fisher. Was it because he was a Black American and working in the area of Barbara's travels or due to the fact that he left Galion without notice? Or was it because he truly was the guilty party?

Regardless of the reasoning, a search for Frank Fisher was on. The Mayor offered and the City Council confirmed the offer of a $100 reward for Fisher's capture.

"The same evening the Mayor issued a reward for the arrest of Fisher, a wise course, and one that had the desired outcome." [23]

A Resolution [24]

To offer a reward for the arrest of the negro who committed the crime of rape upon the person of little Barbara Rettig, April 28th 1882.

Resolved by the city council of the City of Galion, Ohio, that the mayor of said city be and he is hereby authorized to offer a reward of one hundred dollars cash. For the arrest of the negro who committed a crime of rape upon the person of little Barbara Rettig on the 28th day of April AD 1882 at or near the City of Galion.

Resolved that in no case shall the above reward or any part thereof be paid to any person or persons who may have arrested said negro at any time before the passage of this resolution.

Clerk Pro Tem M. Wisler President of the City Council

A CRIMINAL WANTED.

The Mayor of Galion Offers a Reward for the Arrest of Fisher for Rape.

SPECIAL DISPATCH TO THE ENQUIRER.

GALION, OHIO, April 28.—A reward of $100 will be paid for the arrest and delivery of a negro who passes under the name of Frank Fisher. He is very black, bow-legged, about five feet six inches in height, heavy set, with a short mustache and chin-whiskers. When he left Galion he had on a rubber coat, a soft felt hat, well worn and running to a peak, and barefooted. He is wanted for the crime of rape.

ABRAM UNDERWOOD, Mayor of Galion.

Figure 14- Cincinnati Enquirer, April 29, 1882

The *Cincinnati Enquirer* reported on the search for Fisher:

"Twenty-five determined and armed men started in pursuit of the brutal black ravisher, and, if they overtake him, Judge Lynch can add another subject to his list. The entire city and country surrounding is excited and ready to hang or shoot the wretch who has so terribly wrecked a young girl's life. Fisher, the rapist, is a very black negro, with woolly mustache and goatee, and is about five feet six inches in height. It is hoped he be will captured and made to pay the penalty for his horrible crime." [25]

The *Galion Enquirer's* first report of Fisher's capture came from Shelby, Ohio, so Galion's Marshal Blacksten headed to Shelby to take Fisher:

"It was sometime after perpetration of the alleged deed before it became known. As soon, however, as the news reached the city, hundreds of citizens proceeded to the scene of the outrage to learn the particulars. Pursuing parties were immediately organized and struck out in different directions in hot pursuit. Telegrams were sent to all points, and, on Saturday morning, a dispatch was received from Shelby that a negro was captured there who answered the description of the fugitive. Marshal Blacksten boarded the local and proceeded to Shelby. Long before the arrival of No. 11 – the train on which the prisoner was expected to be brought to the city – a dense crowd of determined men had assembled, and in the immediate vicinity of the depot were to be seen hundreds of women and children. The No 11 train arrived, but no Marshal or prisoner were on board. The excitement grew intense, and many expressions not complimentary to the authorities were indulged by several excited individuals, who went so far as accusing the Marshal of taking the prisoner off at Crestline and conveying him to the County Jail at Bucyrus. The No 1 train arrived and off stepped Blacksten, who informed the crowd that the party arrested was not the right man. The crowd would not believe this, and openly accused the Marshal of spiriting away the prisoner, a proceeding that under the circumstances would have been very dangerous for him to pursue, as the people were rife to mete out summary punishment of the culprit and all who interfered with their plans." [26]

The *Marion Star* reported Fisher's capture near Shelby and stated he was taken to Bucyrus on the noon train.

"The negro, Fisher, was captured near Shelby this morning and taken to Bucyrus on the noon train. Over one thousand people gathered at the depot at Shelby and frequent threats of stretching him were made.

3. p. m. - He proves to be the wrong man and was released." [27]

Clearly based on the above report, Marshal Blacksten was aware of the intention to lynch Fisher.

The second report of Fisher's capture was in the area of Upper Sandusky and Lima, Ohio and came from the *Bucyrus Journal*:

"Immediately the community became a fierce blaze of excitement; people departed in every direction from Galion to arrest the wretch; the telegraph sent the news in all directions to surrounding towns, and marshals, constables and citizens were everywhere on the alert watching every negro that happened to be a stranger. Numerous arrests and more numerous reports of arrests were made. In this neighborhood near Nevada at Upper Sandusky and at Lima arrests were made. From Shelby and Mansfield similar reports came. One negro was taken from Lima to Galion only to be released as the wrong man notwithstanding suspicious circumstances indicated that he might be the villain." [28]

An early report from the *St. Louis Dispatch* gave the name of the wrong person for Fisher. Jerry Myers was the owner of land where Frank Fisher was supposedly cutting wood for Mrs. Myers:

"Several hundred men are scouring the vicinity of Galion, searching for a negro American named Jerry Myers, who yesterday brutally ravished a 13 year old girl named Barbara Rettig, whom he found by the roadside, gagged and dragged into the woods. The excitement is intense. If found he will be summarily dispatched." [29]

The *Bucyrus Telegraph Forum* reported that after a Black American arrived in Bucyrus from Galion on early Saturday morning and thought to be Fisher a pursuit was reported. This person turned out to be the same person previously arrested in Upper Sandusky:

"Previous, however, to our (Bucyrus) being notified to be on the lookout, he had passed on through, going west on the track of the Fort Wayne railroad. Soon after a hand-car was pressed into service, and a vigorous pursuit inaugurated. About six miles out he was overtaken but parties from Galion who were among the pursuers failed to recognize him as the man wanted, and he telling a straight story was allowed to go.

Subsequently, the same negro was arrested by Upper Sandusky officers and taken to Galion Sunday morning. In the meantime the Galion authorities received information of the capture of a suspicious appearing negro at Shelby." [30]

The *Ohio State Journal* report out of Upper Sandusky stated:

"Frank Fisher, who is suspected of outraging the little German girl at Galion, was captured by Marshal Grundish two and a half miles east of this place. He, hearing of Fisher coming this way, took a hand car and one or two men and started east, and met the man, who answers the description." [31]

The *Cincinnati Enquirer* reported on the facts related to the Crawford County sheriff heading to Columbus in search of Fisher:

"The Sheriff of Crawford County is here searching for Frank Smith ("colored"), who raped a little girl at Galion yesterday. Smith tried to enlist at the Barracks today, and was seen at several places today. The Sheriff and police have scoured the city for him tonight, but failed to apprehend the fiend. The Sheriff fear he will be lynched if found." [32]

Even more evidence law enforcement officials were aware of the impending lynching.

The pursuit in Columbus was reported in much greater detail in the *Ohio State Journal* as follows:

"The police of this city have been scouring the alleys and dives ever since Saturday afternoon in search of this same Frank Fisher, who seems to be quite a numerous quantity. It was reported that he arrived here Saturday noon in his escape from the enraged citizens of Galion; that he had been seen getting off a street car hastening for Pigeon Roost; that he attempted to enlist at the Barracks, and so on. The officers were making the dust fly in hope of gaining some reputation by the capture of this fiend. The Sheriff of Crawford County was here and from descriptions given they feel convinced that Fisher was in Columbus. All the dives, and especially those kept by "colored" persons, were searched, and the city was hunted over completely. The Sheriff gave out about midnight Saturday night and went to bed for needed rest, as he had been on the rush all day. He left the case with the officers and the search was kept up while burglars, that have kept the city in terror for a month by their numerous depredations, were also at large and none of them captured. The extreme vigilance exercised in this case, which evidently must have been a false chase, naturally suggests the idea that the same earnestness should be practiced in running down the fiends and the thieves that are operating at home." [33]

According to an account of Bill Bloomer published in *The Olentangy Legacy*, for some unexplained reason no one initially searched to the east toward Mansfield, Ohio:

"Posses were formed to scour the county but it appears there was not a directing head. The countryside for miles around was gone over, north, south and west, but unfortunately not in the easterly direction.

As word of the crime spread, greater became the excitement, and threats of vengeance increased. When night closed in, the search was temporarily abandoned. In the meantime, a description of Fisher had been telegraphed to every town and city within a radius of fifty miles and to the city papers as well.

Every officer was on the alert and several suspects brought in. When Saturday dawned, Fisher was still at large, but all Ohio knew of the crime and joined in the search. It was not until 9 o'clock Saturday morning that a clue was obtained when a boy came to town and told of a man answering the description going east. This was later corroborated by a countrywoman who saw him making way on foot toward Mansfield.

Believed to have relatives living in Columbus, Fisher would endeavor to reach them by way of the B & O Railroad and policeman William Nichols and constable Thomas Wurts were dispatched in that direction. By forced driving, the officers reached Fredericktown at midnight where they were joined by Marshal Braddock of that village." [34]

The Capture

After numerous false alarms and false arrests regarding the status of Frank Fisher, turns out, a tip from a young boy leads to his capture, as reported by the *Bucyrus Telegraph Forum*:

> "The first information that led the pursuers on the right track was brought by a small boy who announced that he had seen a man answering Fisher's description on the road leading to the east. The boy's details of the negro's appearance was so life-like that it was felt there could be no mistake. This clue was followed vigorously and officers Wurts and Nichols left at once, going first to Ontario where they learned that a man answering Fisher's description had procured lunch. They then pushed on to Mansfield where they were informed by a famer that the party they were seeking had been seen on the south road. The officer then drove to Fredericktown, Knox County where they hoped to intercept him. There they were joined by the Marshal of the town and the three acted in concert in their search." [35]

The reports of the events in Fredericktown that lead to Fisher's arrest very greatly. One report indicates he was captured while walking along the railroad track, while another claims he was captured while coming out of a barn, heading out of town:

> "The "colored" brute Frank Fisher, who so horribly outraged the little German girl here last week, was caught at Fredericktown yesterday, and brought here this forenoon." [36]

The *Bucyrus Telegraph Forum* reported the capture occurring along a railroad track:

"While walking along the railroad track about five o'clock in the morning they suddenly came face to face with Fisher. Officer Nichols at once recognized him and placed him under arrest." [37]

The *Galion Enquirer* reported the capture occurred in a barn:

"The pursuit was diligently kept up, and the officers of the surrounding towns, who had been notified by telegraph, were on the lookout. About 5 o'clock Sunday morning the rapist was run down at Fredericktown, Knox County, by Officers W. H. W. Nichols and T. J. Wurts, of this city. He was just coming out of a barn and about to leave Fredericktown on foot when he was overhauled. Wurts asked him if his name was Frank Fisher, when he replied "No, sah; that is not my name, sah." Officers Nichols knew him, and, after a few more questions were asked, the officers, as a matter of course arrested him, and at once started with him in a carriage for Galion." [38]

The *Olentangy Legacy* reported the capture as follows:

"At 4 o'clock Sunday morning the officers began the hunt, going north on the railroad track in the hope of intercepting their quarry and the deduction proved to be correct, for they had advanced but a short distance with Marshal Braddock in the lead, when rounding a curve, came face to face with the fugitive. As the other officers hastened up, Officer Nichols placed him under arrest.

Fisher was taken to Fredericktown and Officers Nichols and Wurtz immediately prepared to return the prisoner to Galion. Fisher made no resistance and protested his innocence during the return, to the questioning of Nichols and Wurtz. The party arrived in Galion at 10 o'clock Sunday morning and Fisher lodged behind the bars of the town's jail." [39]

The *Cleveland Leader* reported on the condition of Fisher's underwear:

"This morning about 4 o'clock, Fisher was arrested at Fredericktown, Knox County, by Marshal Braddock of that place. Officers from Galion were upon his track in hot pursuit, and soon appeared on the scene. He was examined, and his underwear gave evidence of his guilt, and he was promptly turned over to the officers from this place." [40]

"Frank Fisher, the "colored" fiend who committed an outrage on the thirteen year old Rettig girl near Galion last Friday, was captured here by Marshal Braddock, of this place, at 4 o'clock this morning, and was fully identified by Night Policeman Nichols, who was in hot pursuit. The wretch's underclothing gave conclusive evidence of his guilt. The officers have taken him back to Galion." [41]

The *Bucyrus Journal* reported Fisher's arrest by Marshal Braddock:

"Officers Nichols and Wurtz of Galion had received news from Marshal Lemon, of Mansfield that caused them to go to Fredericktown, Knox Co., and here, on the railroad, coming around curve about 4 o'clock on Sunday morning, he was arrested by Marshal Braddock of Fredericktown, and identified by the Galion officers who were with Braddock and to whom Fisher was known. The miserable brute was at once taken in a buggy to Galion where he arrived about 11 o'clock.

Immediately a large and excited crowd collected but after a while dispersed. The man had been brought in somewhat privately, although no special secrecy was attempted, but the people expected the man arrested at Lima was the fellow and be was expected from Crestline, consequently the main part of the crowd were at the depot, and the throng was so dense that the train had to stop before it reached the depot." [42]

The *Cincinnati Enquirer* on plans to move Fisher from the City Hall jail:

"The prisoner was at once taken to the jail in the City Hall and confined in one of the heavy iron cages, and the Mayor and city officers were laying plans to take him to the County Jail at Bucyrus, or some other jail in some neighboring County, fearing that the loud threats of lynching would be carried out if Fisher should remain in the City Hall cell." [43]

The *Cincinnati Enquirer* reported Fisher was captured by Galion officers Wurts and Nichols:

"Frank Fisher was captured about five o'clock this morning at Fredericktown, Knox County, by Officers T. J. Wurts and W. H. W. Nichols, of this city. The arrest was, made just as the negro was about to leave Fredericktown on foot. He was first accosted by Officer Wurts, who asked him whether his name was not Frank Fisher. "No, sah, that is net my name sah." he replied, but Officer Nichols knew him, and after a few more questions, among which was asked why be bad left Galion, he replied that he had got tired of chopping wood, and thought lie would skip. The officers, of course, arrested him, and at once started with him in a carriage, accompanied by two Fredericktown officers, for this city, arriving here at half-past ten this morning." [44]

The *Bucyrus Telegraph Forum* also reported on the condition of Fisher's underclothing:

"Fisher was asked why he left Galion and replied that he was dissatisfied with his work. An examination of his underclothing saturated with blood. This he accounted for by saying that his nose had been bleeding, but just why he should wipe the blood from his face with the caudal appendage of his nether garment he did not attempt to explain." [45]

The *Cleveland Leader* reported on the arrest and the gathering of the crowds at the jail:

"The news of his arrest spread like wildfire, and the people began to gather in excited crowds in different parts of the town. Shortly after locomotive whistles were sounded and the fire bells rang, when moved by a common impulse, some six or seven hundred people made a rush for the jail, "colored" and white men vying with each other in their eagerness to revenge the terrible outrage. The sheriff was wholly unprepared for the assault and protests and pleadings were in vain." [46]

EYEWITNESS BILL SPONHAUER:

"The mob was led by a group of "galvanizers" from the New York Central yards. This group broke into the jail first and several of the men had guard Bill Nichols by the throat and were choking him "until his tongue was hanging out," ordering him to give them the key to the cell. He finally gave in and got the key from under the coal bucket where he had hidden it. The cell was unlocked and in any case, the prisoner was in the hands of the crowd. He was pulled out from under the bunk where he had hidden and hurried out into the street." [47]

It should be noted that William Sponhauer was born June 19, 1875, so he was not yet seven years old at the time of the alleged rape.

Figure 15 - City Building and Opera House

There are conflicting reports regarding which jail Fisher was placed in. One option was the jail located in the city hall/opera house building located at the southeast corner of South Liberty Street and East Main Street (now Harding Way East) the location of the current city hall building.

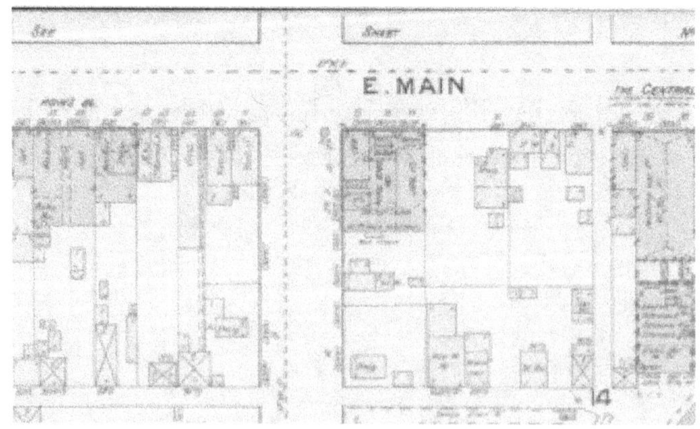

Figure 16 - City Hall Location

The other option was the fire station and jail located at West Atwood Street (now a vacant lot at 116 W. Atwood Street). The jail at the City Building is the more likely of the two options.

Figure 17- Atwood Street Fire St

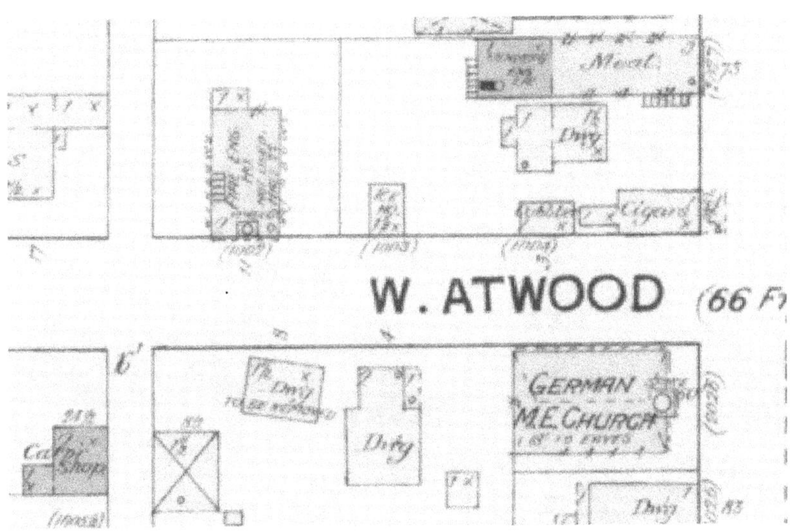

Figure 18- Atwood Street Fire Station Location

An important question that will likely never be answered is why the Galion officers, knowing the calls for Fisher's demise, would take him to Galion. Based on reports of concern about Fisher's safety in Galion plans were being made to take him to a neighboring jail so there was widespread knowledge of the risk of taking Fisher to Galion.

They had previous contact with Marshal Lemon of Mansfield and had to pass close by Mansfield on their way from Fredericktown to Galion. Fisher could have been taken to the Mansfield of Richland County jails.

The Lynching

What happens to the human body during a lynching has been the subject of fairly extensive research. Some information has come from survivors of attempted lynching. Below is a summary of the impact of lynching on the human body:

The victim sees flashes of white and blackness and falls into a feeling of weakness and powerlessness. A full minute passes before they loses consciousness. Their body convulses several times. There are spasmodic and uncoordinated rippling movements of their limbs. Their chest heaves as they gasps their last breath. In five minutes they are brain dead. In another ten minutes their heart stops beating.

Their face becomes engorged and livid as the brain is filled with blood which cannot get back out. There are signs little blood marks on their face and their eyes from burst blood capillaries due to excessive blood pressure in their head. Their tongue protrudes due to the pressure of the noose on the base of it. Their face turns pale and bluish in colour.

As with the pursuit and capture, the lynching of Frank Fisher was described in various detail by the newspapers across the country. Crowds were reported to be from 2,000 to 5,000.

The *Cleveland Leader* reported:

"The sight was a most disgraceful one. On either side of Fisher were men much his superior in size, and all the distance from the jail to the girl's home he was choked and kicked at almost every step. During all this excitement the fire bell had rung repeatedly, but no heed was given the call, many thinking it was only a ruse to attract the attention of the mob. On the way down South Market Street, though, it was discovered that a fire really was in progress. A small frame dwelling was on fire. The fire engine was there but no one to run it, and as a result the building was burned.

When the mob with Fisher in charge arrived at the home of the girl. He was taken into her presence and identified by her. She seemed very much frightened on seeing him. The evidence was very conclusive from beginning to end that they had the right man, and the determination to hang him seemed greater than before. He was immediately taken to the woods where he committed the deed. For some reason a suitable place seemed hard to find and he was marched from one end of the woods to the other two or three times. Finally the right place was found.

His arms and legs were pinioned, a handkerchief placed upon his face, the rope adjusted, and the poor black man was swung away from the earth and earthly misery. It is estimated that at least three thousand people witnessed the hanging, a great many having arrived from Crestline, Bucyrus, and other neighboring towns." [48]

The *Cleveland Leader* reported Fisher choked to death:

"Frank Fisher, the negro who ravished a thirteen-year-old girl Friday was lynched at Galion at 4 o'clock this afternoon by a mob of about 200 men. Fisher made no resistance, and while hanging squirmed but once. He choked to death." [49]

The *Ohio State Journal* reported on the hanging in detail as follows:

"Arrangements were being made to send him to jail in some neighboring County to prevent the threatened lynching, at three o'clock a crowd of determined men, unmasked, went to the City Hall Prison and demanded him. The officers refused, and Mayor Underwood and others made speeches to them, counseling that the law be permitted to take its course, but the mob forced the doors, broke open the cage and dragged the negro into the street with fierce shouts.

Meanwhile a delegation, accompanied by a physician who had been pressed into service, drove to the house of the victim to ascertain whether the girl, Barbara Rettig, was mentally and physically able to confront and identify the negro. She told them she could, as she had often seen him chopping wood. This being reported to the crowd, the negro was marched there, preceded by men carrying a rope, and surrounded by a howling mob. When she saw the cowering negro she said, "That's the man," and fainted.

The noose was then thrown over his head, and he was dragged to a tree at the rear of the lot. Somebody suggested the scene of the outrage as the best place to strangle him. This met the view of all, and Fisher was taken to the spot, where he was told his time had come to die. He protested his innocence to the last, but the blood still on his clothes was evidence of his guilt, as well as the girl's statement. He prayed, "O Lord, take care of me! I know I'm going to die. I have no friends." The remainder of his prayer was drowned in shouts. His hands were tied behind his back, a handkerchief put over his face, and he was strung up at 4:10 p. m. The body was still hanging as a late hour." [50]

The *Marion Star* gave names of participants:

"Several Marion people were present at the Galion Nigger Hangin' yesterday and we learned that some 2,000 people witnessed the execution. It is said the "black mocking bird" Bruce climbed the first tree to tie the rope, and that Sam Smith, a former typo at the STAR office climbed the second tree, where the deed was done." [51]

The *Columbus Dispatch* also reported on the lynching in detail:

"At about 2:30 pm the alarm of fire was given, which brought every citizen to the rescue, thinking that it was only a sham to get a mob to lynch the negro. There really was a fire in the south part of town, but, when those who would have protected Fisher had gone to the fire, another gang organized, went to the calaboose, knocked down the doors, seized the prisoner and took him to the girl who had been ravished for identification. She recognized him at once, as did several others, which was sufficient to convince the mob that they had the right man.

The crowd then marched down to the woods where the crime was committed, tied a handkerchief over his face and strung him up to an iron tree in the presence of two thousand people, mob and all unmasked.

About five thousand people went down to take a look at the body while it was hanging, waiting to be cut down by the coroner." [52]

The *Cleveland Leader* reported:

"Fisher was dragged out by the infuriated mob. He was taken to the bedside of the victim, who instantly identified him as the person who had outraged her. The crowd had in the meantime rapidly swelled, until it now numbered between two and three thousand. The terrified creature was roughly seized by the leaders and taken towards the woods where the outrage was committed, followed by the excited crowd, uttering curses and threats of vengeance in his ears. Arriving upon the scene Fisher was given Five Minutes to Make His Peace which the doomed man devoted in appeals to God for mercy, and in protesting his innocence of the horrible crime. During this time the mod stood comparatively quiet, but evidently impatient for the execution of their victim. At the end of the allotted time a rope was adjusted about the neck, and he was swung up, and left hanging until he was dead. After which the crowd slowly dispersed and the body was left hanging to the tree where it remained up to half past 9 o'clock tonight. The mayor and other officers did all in their power to check the frenzied multitude, but they were powerless to enforce obedience to the law, and their entreaties were unheeded. Many of our best people condemn the act and deplore the unwarranted exhibition of lawlessness. [53]

The *Cincinnati Enquirer* reported in even greater detail:

"Their fears were well founded, for the news of Fisher's capture spread through the city and neighboring towns like wildfire, and at three o'clock this afternoon a large crowd of determined men, boldly, defiantly and unmasked, with hammers, crowbars and other implements of demolition and a huge and significant looking rope, presented themselves before the entrance of the City Hall Prison and demanded that Frank Fisher, the negro rapist, be surrendered into their hands. The officers of the Court refused. Then ensued a terrible scene of strife. The handful of officers were powerless, and the speeches of Mayor Underwood, G.M. Zeagler and others, who begged the excited crowd to let the law take its course and deal with the prisoner whose blood they sought, were unavailing and unheard. With their implements of destruction they forced open the doors as though they were paper, broke open the iron cage that contained the guilty, trembling wretch, and, grasping him with a dozen hands as in a vise, they pulled him out into the street with a defiant shout.

Previous to this, however, a delegation, accompanied by a physician whom they had pressed into service, drove furiously down to the residence of the victim of the negro's lust to ascertain whether she was in a proper mental and physical condition to see the negro for identification. The physician state to your correspondent that he asked her whether she knew the negro who caused her misery. She replied yes; that she had often seen him while he was chopping wood near their home, and described his appearance; and, being asked whether she could identify him, she replied that she could.

The delegation satisfied, reported at once at the City Hall, and then the scene that has been described was enacted. With hoots, yells and cheers the crowd, preceded by some men and boys bearing the fatal rope, marched with the frightened negro monster to the Rettig residence at the foot of South Market street, just at the south city limits, and took the black beast into the presence of Barbara Rettig, the little girl whom he had so horribly outraged. As soon as her eyes fell upon the cowardly and cowering wretch before her, she exclaimed, "That is the man who did it," and soon fainted with the terrible recollections. The crowd threw the rope over the negro's head and dragged him to a tree in the rear of the lot, but someone suggested the woods, the scene of the terrible crime, hard by, at the fit place to expiate his crime, and to the woods where he had been but a few days ago chopping wood, Frank Fisher was dragged and told his time to die had come. He protested his innocence to the last, but the blood stains upon his clothing and the girl's evidence, coupled with his numerous lies to the officers, were enough to condemn him in the minds of the infuriated and desperate crowd, and hang him. They argued that a trial by law would only send him to the Penitentiary and cheat the gallows of as black-hearted a demon as ever trod the earth, but they let him pray for a short time. He said his prayer: "O Lord take care of me; I know that I am going to die, but I have many friends."

The balance of his appeal was drowned by the cries of the crowd to string him up. His hands were tied behind his back, his feet pinioned, a handkerchief placed over his face, a steady pull was given on the rope, 1the end made fast to a stump, and at ten minutes past four o'clock the soul of Frank Fisher, the negro rapist, was sent to answer for his crime before a higher Court that that of Crawford County, and at this writing (9 o'clock p.m.) his body still dangles in mid-air.

It is estimated that at least two thousand people, men, women and children, among whom was your correspondent, witnessed the execution by Judge Lynch. A large number of people from Bucyrus, Mount Gilead, Crestline and other neighboring towns witnessed the ghastly spectacle.

We should have stated that while the negro was being taken by the crowd a fire alarm was sounded, and the lynchers thought it a ruse to get them to disperse. But the alarm was genuine. A frame house on South Market Street in the line of march to the woods, having caught fire." [54]

THE MOB LYNCHING OF FRANK FISHER

The *Cleveland Plain Dealer* reported on the mob taking Fisher to Ms. Rettig's home:

"Immediately a crowd began to gather and ominous threats of lynching were heard. The fire bells were sounded, whistles blown, and the people began to gather around the jail. The officers in charge of the jail were unprepared for an assault and tried to induce the mob to leave. The Mayor also addressed the mob, advising order and counseling them to let the law take its course. All pleadings were vain. A rush was made, the jail doors forced, the prisoner's cell broken into and the hapless wretch dragged out, howling and begging for mercy. The people seemed frenzied with fury and the prisoner was dragged along the street, kicked, choked and pelted with stones at every step.

The negro was taken to the home of the injured girl and taken into her presence, as she lay suffering the most intense pain, and unable to move. She was asked if the prisoner was the man who misused her and she said without hesitation that he was the man. There was other and conclusive evidence against him, and he was told that his time had come to die. He was taken from the house and followed by a howling mob of at least two thousand people, dragged to the woods where his crime was committed and bidden to make his peace with God for his time was short. He was told he could have five minutes to pray, but all the more he writhed and twisted and asked for mercy. To the very last he declared his innocence. When the five minutes had expired the hands of the shrieking wretch were pinioned, a rope was placed around his neck and the other end thrown over the limb of a tree. There was a moment's pause and pitiful scream of the victim was stifled as the rope was pulled up and he swung writhing in mid-air. The crowd stood by until the last convulsive struggles were over and then disappeared, leaving the body hanging, and where it remained all night." [55]

The *Bucyrus Journal* reported on the mob:

"After a while, however it became known that the criminal had been brought in a buggy from Fredericktown, and that he was in the lockup, to which place the excitement was immediately transferred. Without any attempt at concealment, defying the Mayor, deaf to all protests from prominent citizens, the Marshal and his assistant were overpowered, the calaboose was broken open, the cell or iron cage in which the fellow was confined was wrenched open and he was dragged out and a rope put around his neck.

Either to gain time or to be certain, a committee and a physician were sent in a carriage to the residence of the suffering child to ascertain if she were in a condition to recognize the man; and having returned with an affirmative answer, the criminal was hauled, kicked, knocked and otherwise driven there where he arrived more dead than alive. The suffering child recognized the man and fainted and be was then taken to the scene of his crime. Here five minutes were given him for prayer, but the infuriated mob, before two minutes were gone, clamored for his life; some one climbed a tree and put the rope over and fainting and insensible the ravisher was drawn up, and with scarcely struggle, strangled to death denying his crime to the last." [56]

The *Bucyrus Telegraph Forum* gave an extensive report:

"So soon as the intelligence of the capture spread throughout the city, the excitement which had to some extent quieted down was renewed with five-fold intensity. Crowds gathered in the vicinity of the prison, and the authorities realized that a serious outbreak was liable to occur. As the hours passed, the crowd grew in dimensions and the determination to wreak summary vengeance upon the prisoner increased in proportion. Usually, mobs are ineffective by reason of the lack of leadership. On this occasion however, there was no difficulty of the kind. Each of the perhaps one thousand men present was willing and anxious to take the lead.

THE MOB LYNCHING OF FRANK FISHER

It is but just to say that Mayor Underwood did all in his power to restrain the mob. In the midst of jeers, denunciation and cries of "Hang the brute!" "Bring a rope!" "Break open the door!" etc., the Mayor endeavored to make himself heard arguing, pleading and beseeching the crowd to disperse and allow the law to take its course. He was followed by ex-Prosecutor George M. Zeigler to whom the crowd refused to listen. Several of the infuriated citizens replied briefly, declaring amid shouts of approval that no man's family was safe so long as such brutes as Fisher were permitted to live. Suddenly a determined rush was made, and in a moment the door of the prison gave way and after a brief resistance by Officers Nichols and Wurts, who were on the inside, the prisoner was seized and a rope procured from a fire engine in the same building placed about his neck and he dragged and hustled into the street.

The excitement became intensified, each member of the mob essaying to reach the prisoner and deal to him his share of the demand for vengeance. It seemed that Pandemonium had broken loose, the cries of the mob mingling with the shrill shrieks of locomotive whistles and the clang of the fire bells. It is probable that Fisher would have been killed then and there had it not been for the orders of some cooler heads who demanded that the attacks upon the prisoner should cease; that they proposed to hang the miscreant and not beat him to death. At this time the streets were filled by a mass of surging humanity, in which women and children mingled with excited men. The hour was about three o'clock and the afternoon Sunday schools adjourned in response to the prevailing excitement, added their numbers to the crowd, and for the time being the salutary lessons of meek forgiveness were smothered by the thirst for blood. The prisoner made no outcry and seemed to be dazed and bewildered by the horror of his position.

A body guard of the most determined men was formed and the tumultuous procession moved rapidly toward prisoner's victim, the object being to place him before her for identification. The intervening distance was soon traversed and Fisher was taken into the house where the girl was resting in bed. She gave him one searching look and with the cry, "That is the man!" sank back with horror and passed into a swoon. The prisoner was hurried from the house and the announcement made to the waiting crowd that he had been identified. This was received with a savage cry which could be likened to nothing so much as the fierce blood-curdling growl of the tiger as he springs upon his victim. A low piece of ground on the Myers farm was first selected as the place of execution but at the suggestion of some one the scene was removed nearer to the point where the outrage was committed. There within one hundred yards of the road and near the railroad track, a tree was selected and around it the crowd gathered. An ominous stillness fell upon the scene as the prisoner was led beneath the gallows and it was announced by one of the leaders that he would be given five minutes to pray. The wretch fell upon his knees and for a few minutes unctuously beseeched the Lord to have mercy upon his soul. So far he had made no approach to a confession further than a remark that be dropped after being identified to the effect that he was drunk at the time. In his prayer he asked that the Almighty might forgive him the sin if he was guilty. His prayer was interrupted by another howl of rage, and he was assisted to his feet, after which, with painful deliberation, his feet were tied, his hands pinioned behind him and a handkerchief drawn over his face. Not a word of protest was uttered by the wretch beyond the single exclamation that it was wrong to hang an innocent man. A boy had in the meantime climbed the tree and adjusted the rope. At a given signal a score of eager hands clutched the other end of the cord, and the victim of the mob's vengeance was jerked several feet in the air. The end of the rope was fastened to an adjacent tree, and with blanched faces and bated breath the crowd watched the dying struggles of their victim. His death struggles were not violent, and beyond a convulsive shudder, a spasmodic contraction of the legs and labored heaving of the breast there was nothing to indicate that the cord of life was being torn asunder. Satisfied with their horrid work, the crowd among which were scores of well-dressed women and children, quietly dispersed leaving the body hanging." [57]

Like the BTF, the *Galion Inquirer* reported in great detail:

"The news of the arrest spread rapidly, and soon the City Hall was surrounded by an excited and desperate crowd of citizens of all stations of life. Threats of lynching were so freely indulged in that the officers laid plans to take the prisoner to the County jail at Bucyrus, or some other jail in some neighboring County. Mayor Underwood, Geo. M. Ziegler and others tried to reason with the crowd, telling them that the girl was in such a precarious condition it would not be safe to take the ravisher to be identified, and urging them to proceed to no violence, but to allow the prisoner to remain where he was until morning, at such time as the doctor in attendance said it would be safe for his patient to identify Fisher.

The more excited ones of the crowd yelled out, "Hang him! Hang him!" and made for the prison door. But a proposition was made by one in the crowd to appoint a committee to proceed to the house of the victim and satisfy themselves is she was in a condition to recognize the negro. This proposition was quickly acted upon, and a committee of four was appointed. They returned in about half an hour, when a spokesman arose in his seat in the wagon and addressed the crowd. "The girl," he said, "is quite ill, but she says she is willing to recognize the negro today." At this announcement a loud and piercing shout went up from the vast crowd demanding the authorities give up the prisoner, saying no action would be taken until after he was recognized by the victim. This was refused.

The scene that followed beggars description, and was terrible to behold. At this moment the alarm of fire was from the Atwood street engine-house. It was considered a ruse to disperse the crowd, and, in our opinion, hastened the action of the crowd. It, however, was correct, as a frame dwelling near the house of Rettig had caught on fire, and was partially consumed. Someone shook the door of the prison, when the cry went up: "Down with it!" and in less time than it takes us to write it the doors were forced open, and the howling, yelling mob flocked into the room. The officers fought bravely, but what could they do against such a crowd? They demanded the key of the cell from officers Nichols, but not getting it they proceeded to batter down the cell, the officers meanwhile being cornered and held firmly by some of the lynchers. Hammers and bars of iron were brought into requisition, and soon the lock was broken from the door, and with a shout of triumph the poor, trembling, horrified wrench was pulled from under the bunk, where he, in is terror, had crawled and was unceremoniously hurried into the street.

The entire populace seemed to have gone crazy, and the scene presented in front of the prison and in the neighborhood that Sunday afternoon was one that has never before been witnessed in the history of Crawford County, and one that causes a shudder of horror when thought of. Strong and by no means kind hands seized the negro, and he was hurried along toward the home of his victim, the crowd, which numbered about three thousand, following, hooting and yelling, and one of the number swinging a rope over his head.

Recognized in due time the home of Rettig, which is on South Market street, just outside the corporate limits, was reached, and the prisoner brought before the victim, who was confined to her bed. She raised up her head and, looking the cringing, trembling wretch square in the face, said: "That is the man!" No sooner were the words than the father struck a powerful blow at the negro, but he was so suddenly jerked back that the blow fell harmless.

The same parties who first seized the negro never let him go, and he was dragged from the presence of his victim to the front yard and then to the rear of the lot, where there was a tree. At a suggestion of someone, the doomed man was marched to the scene of the outrage.

Before reaching the fatal tree a halt was made and some questions asked the culprit. Even now he denied his guilt, and gave trivial excuses for his running away. The crowd, becoming impatient at the delay, kept up their cry of "Hang him!" The fatal tree was soon reached, when the now almost dead and doomed man was given five minutes for prayer. "O Lord," he commenced, "take care of me. I know that I am going to die, but I have many friends." No more could be heard, as the noise of the crowd drowned his words. His legs and arms were then pinioned, the rope put around his neck, his face covered with a handkerchief, and a 3:40 p.m. was run up to the limb of a tree. There was no struggling or convulsing of the muscles of the chest or limbs, but it seemed as if life had left the body before the rope had tightened around the neck, which was not broken." [58]

The *Cincinnati Enquirer* reported on the removal of Fisher's body from the tree and the coroner's refusal to come to the site of the hanging:

"The last act in yesterday's terrible tragedy, wherein Frank Fisher, the negro who so brutally and horribly outraged the little German girl, Barbara Rettig, lost his life by hanging by a crowd of infuriated men, has not yet closed. The body of the negro, remained suspended in mid-air upon the limb of the tree all night, and two fires were kept burning by some persons delegated by the Mayor to watch the corpse, as it was supposed the Coroner would put in an appearance and hold an inquest.

The Coroner, Phillip Moffat, lives at Bucyrus, a distance of twelve miles, and, as the law does not compel him to go over ten miles to perform his official duties, he has refused to act in this case; consequently this morning Mayor Underwood, accompanied by, Officers Wurtz and Nichols, repaired to the woods, cut down the lawless monster and brought him to the City Hall Prison, from which he had been torn by the enraged populace yesterday, and placed his remains upon a bunk in an iron cage, where hundreds of people have gazed upon them to-day. They were this evening taken in charge by the Township Trustees, and will be buried tomorrow." [59]

GALION POLICE REPORT:

"The crime occurred on April 28 and the accused was captured on Sunday morning the 30th. Upon return of the prisoner to Galion by members of this department, a mob of around 3000 people later in the day overpowered the Marshal and his deputies and removed the prisoner from the city jail." [60]

WALTER HESSENAUER REPORT:

"I had gone to Dayton, Ohio, with the Rotary Club to a meeting and was approached by the storyteller after he learned that I was from the Midwest City of Galion, Ohio. He introduced himself as being formerly from the city of Galion and struck up a conversation with the words that follow:

I want to tell you a story that I am sure not many people in your city would be able to repeat and that is when I was a young boy, there were a large number of saloons in Galion (he gave the number) and one hotel. The saloons were well attended on weekends.

There had been talk of an incident on a Friday and rapidly circuited the saloons and spread through the town. The story increased with each telling about a man molesting a young girl on the County Line Road. Matters were being compounded from saloon to saloon all day Saturday so that by Sunday morning, a large crowd had gathered and become out of control at the town jail, located near the spot where Wilson Printing Company now stands at the intersection of Market and Atwood Streets.

The church where I attended Sunday school and the jail were at the same location near this corner. While I attended Sunday school on that fateful Sunday there was considerable excitement outside the

THE MOB LYNCHING OF FRANK FISHER

Sunday school, and as the activity was getting louder with a great amount of noise, it was very hard for the children to obey rules and to stay in their seats.

The Sunday school teacher made attempts to quiet the children and to make them keep their seats but as the noise grew louder, some of us attempted to see from the window, and while the teacher was occupied with this, I snuck out and observed firsthand the events as they happened.

The prisoner was removed from the jail and was tied behind a farm wagon and the procession proceeded south on Market Street toward the County Line Road. As the procession proceeded south to a point approximately at the intersection of South Boston Street a fire crew responding to a fire caused the procession to move aside for the crew to pass.

[An idea of the time frame in which this scene was taking place can be more appreciated when the storyteller explained that the fire engine was a hand pumper and was pulled by the crew].

The location or details of the fire were not revealed to me and have little significance to the outcome of this story.

The crowd stopped at the home of the family of the child that was involved in the tragic event.

The father came out and made an attempt to explain to the crowd that the child was not harmed in any way but was only very frightened as she had never seen a man of that color before.

The father, being of German descent, could not speak very good English and the gathering was by this time out of control and would not be deterred from the task they had set out to accomplish."

Important, previously unreported, facts regarding the statements attributed to Walter Hessenauer include his family connection to the Rettig family.

Walter Hessenauer's parents were Henry J Hessenauer and Margaret Rettig. Margaret Rettig's parents were Peter Rettig and Eva Boehm. Margaret's sister was Barbara Rettig. Margaret was 3 years older than Barbara and would have been very aware of the alleged rape of her sister.

If would be reasonable to assume that Walter Hessenauer's report regarding the rape of Barbara Rettig was information provided by his mother Margaret Hessenauer (older sister of Barbara Rettig) and not information he gleaned from a conversation with a stranger in Dayton, Ohio.

The story of Walter Hessenuaer, therefore, should be given significant credibility.

The Burial

Fisher's burial was reported in various detail. It appears his body ended up in the Fairview Cemetery as part of moving the Union Green Cemetery internments.

"On Tuesday morning the last act in the tragedy was performed and the body of Fisher was taken to the cemetery and interred in obscure corner with only a board inscribed with his name to mark the spot." [61]

"Corner (Bauer) refused to hold an inquest, and the body was turned over to the County Trustees for burial. The remains were taken to the Union Green Cemetery early Tuesday morning and buried in Potter's field." [62]

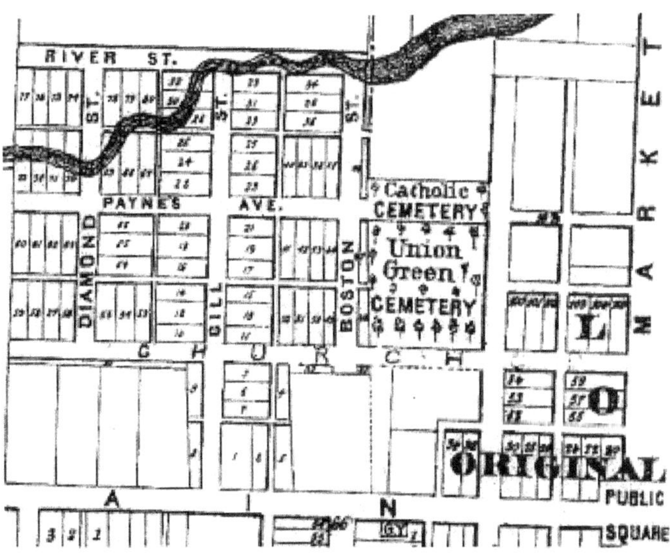

Figure 19 - Union Green Cemetery, Galion, Ohio

"The body hung close to the railroad until after 9 o'clock. Monday. Coroner Moffit, of Bucyrus, was sent for and declined to attend the distance being over ten miles and the Mayor and officers after nine o'clock on Monday went to the place and cut him down and had him buried at the public expense." [63]

"The body of Frank Fisher, the "colored" rapist, who was hanged here by the people, was buried yesterday. No relatives or friends claimed the body and it was buried at city expense." [64]

"The remains of Frank Fisher, the negro rapist hung by Judge Lynch Sunday were buried early this morning by the Township Trustees." [65]

"Long after the body was dangling in mid-air did the crowd linger around, and hundreds of those who had not witnessed the execution, and strangers who came in on the evening trains, were flocking to and from the scene of the tragedy until long after dark. Upon the arrival of the early morning trains Monday morning the body still dangled from the limb where it was suspended, and the trains slacked up to give passengers an opportunity to view the body and surroundings." [66]

"The body was cut down about 10 a.m., and conveyed to the city jail and placed in cell No. 1, facing the door, and was visited by many before the doors were closed against sight-seers. There it lay in all its hideousness – the rope still around the neck, the arms and legs pinioned, and the face uncovered. It was a sickening sight, and caused a shudder of disgust to permeate all who viewed it." [67]

The following morning, by order of the Mayor, the body was cut down and taken to the City Hall where it lay "in state" during the day and was visited by hundreds of curious people. The appearance of the corpse was natural presenting little evidence of a violent death. The eyes were tightly closed and beyond a great contraction of the lower lip the face seemed like that of an ordinary corpse." [68]

THE MOB LYNCHING OF FRANK FISHER

An attempt to take Fisher's body for scientific research was turned back by one Polk Township Trustee.

"W.C. Craven, M.D., Demonstrator of Anatomy in the medical department of the University of Wooster, located in Cleveland, appeared bearing a written and certified requisition Charles C. Arms, M.D., Professor of Anatomy at the same institution, for the body of Frank Fisher. Dr. Craven laid the matter before Mayor Underwood and City Solicitor DeGolly, both of whom decided that, under the law of Ohio regulating the obtaining of bodies for dissection, the Township Trustees were compelled to turn the body over to him, but one of the gentlemen obstinately refused to give his consent, while the other two were favorably disposed. Dr. Craven did everything in his power to carry out his mission, but failed, and returned to Cleveland on the No. 4 today upon receipt of a telegram from Prof. Arms to return if he could not get peaceable possession of the body." [69]

"Parties from Cleveland were in Galion Wednesday endeavoring to procure the body and it is possible he has graced the dissecting table." [70]

"The feeling growing out of the refusal growing out of the refusal of one of the Township Trustees to peacefully give up the body of Frank Fisher to W. C. Craven, M.D., of Cleveland, as announced last week, gave rise to the rumor that the body had been disposed of and was not buried, as stated. To give color to the story, it was reported that Adam Wurts and P. Herbold, the undertaker, had taken the body out of the city prison and buried it at 5 o'clock a.m., when Trustee John C. Beltz prevailed upon the other two Trustees to consent to an investigation of the matter. In accordance with arrangements made, Mr. Beltz, Marshal Blacksten and several others proceeded to the cemetery Tuesday afternoon and had the grave opened. Upon opening the coffin the ghastly object was found therein, thus putting an end to all dispute as to the proper burial of the remains of Frank Fisher." [71]

The Reward Dispute

The dispute between Galion officers and the Fredericktown Marshal over the reward resulted in a bloody fight at the Central Hotel.

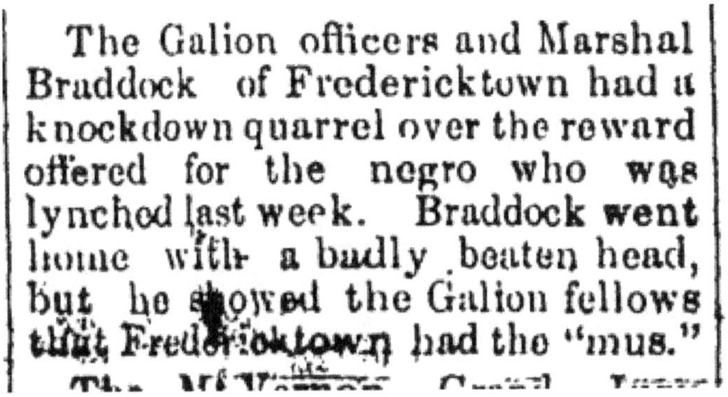

The Galion officers and Marshal Braddock of Fredericktown had a knockdown quarrel over the reward offered for the negro who was lynched last week. Braddock went home with a badly beaten head, but he showed the Galion fellows that Fredericktown had the "mus."

Figure 20- The Bellville Star, May 11, 1882

"In the older days of the drama a tragedy was always succeeded by a farce so as to send the audience home in a good humor. The lynching of Fisher was followed by a roaring farce. On Monday, while Officer Nichols was explaining his connection with the arrest to a friend Marshal Braddock, of Fredericktown, who was present, called him a liar and in response to Nichol's display of belligerency reached for him. The Marshal is a large heavy man and was proceeding to dust all that part of the city with Galion policeman's anatomy when Wurts the partner of Nichols came to the rescue of the latter and used his mace with considerable effect upon the head of Braddock. The combatants were finally separated and blood ceased to flow. The primary cause of the trouble was a difficulty regarding the division of the reward of $100 offered by the Mayor of Galion for the apprehension of Fisher. The latter question is still undisposed of." [72]

"To add to the terrible scenes following the lynching of Fisher, a brawl must occur among the officers over the reward for the capture of the ravisher. An altercation occurred at the Central in this particular between Officer Nichols, of this city, and Marshal Braddock, of Fredericktown.

Figure 21 - The Central Hotel, Galion, Ohio

Both claimed to have made the arrest and the lie was given, when Nichols jumped for and struck at Braddock. The latter is a powerful man, and held Nichols at arm's length and said he did not want to hurt him. They scuffled around for a short time, when Nichols called on Officer T.J. Wurts to assist him. Wurts in a brutal manner, struck Braddock over the head several times with his mace, inflicting severe and dangerous wounds. We have been told by many present, from whom we gained the above particulars of the case, that Braddock was also struck in the head by the but-end of a pistol. Two or three of the wounds inflicted were of such a serious nature as to require the aid of a surgeon to sew them up. The whole affair is denounced as a disgraceful outrage upon Braddock, who, it is claimed, acted the gentleman throughout his stay in our city. It certainly reflects no credit upon officers Nichols and Wurts, and the feeling is strong and outspoken against the latter, who is bitterly denounced for his brutal and unprovoked attach. Braddock and his friends, we are informed, intend taking the matter before the grand jury." [73]

Evidently more than one readers of the Cincinnati Enquirer from Fredericktown took exception to the reporting regarding the dispute over the reward.

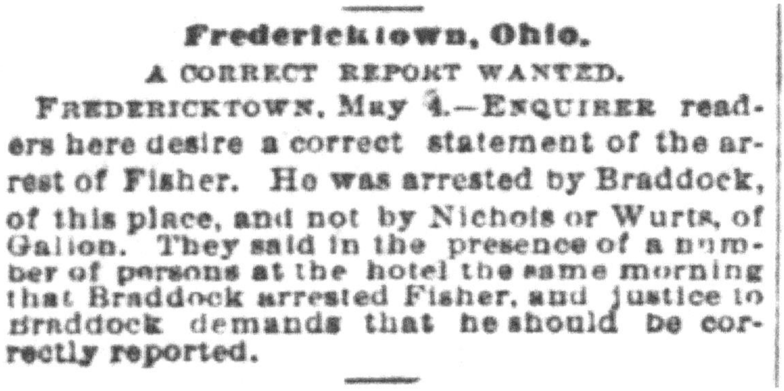

Fredericktown, Ohio.
A CORRECT REPORT WANTED.
FREDERICKTOWN, May 4.—ENQUIRER readers here desire a correct statement of the arrest of Fisher. He was arrested by Braddock, of this place, and not by Nichols or Wurts, of Galion. They said in the presence of a number of persons at the hotel the same morning that Braddock arrested Fisher, and justice to Braddock demands that he should be correctly reported.

Figure 22- Cincinnati Enquirer, May 5, 1882

"A disgraceful scene in the final act was witnessed at the Central Hotel at noon to-day. It seems that Marshal Braddock, of Fredericktown, lays claim to the arrest of Fisher, the rapist, and to-day, when told by Officer Nichols that his claim was false, the two officers got into a knock-down argument. Nichols called for Officer Wurtz, who too hastily used his mace upon Braddock, while the latter and Nichols were mopping the floor with each other, and Braddock was badly cut upon the head in several places by Wurtz's club. One hundred dollars was offered by the City Council for the arrest of Fisher, and therein was the bone of contention.

Your correspondent is informed that the participants in this disgraceful fight will be brought before the Mayor or a Justice tomorrow morning, given a chance to tell their tales, and receive their reward for fighting. The reward of $100 will be paid when it is determined or proved who actually did, make the arrest. The hotel scene is greatly deplored by all our citizens, and nearly all express the opinion that Marshall Braddock is, no doubt, entitled to at least a part of the reward offered for Fisher's arrest." [74]

"The Mayor of Galion had offered a hundred dollars reward for the arrest of the man, and as a fit sequel to this deplorable outrage the officers of Galion on Monday quarreled with Marshal Braddock, of Fredericktown, about their respective rights to the reward, and the Galion officers, two upon one assaulted and beat him very severely." [75]

"The reward for his capture has not yet been paid, as the three officers who had a hand in the arrest have quarreled and fought over the matter as to who is entitled to the reward. Marshal Braddock left for his home at Fredericktown last night, where the arrest was made. The City Council will investigate and pay the reward to the proper person or persons." [76]

The Cincinnati Enquirer concluded Wurts and Nichols were entitled to the reward very early:

"The reward of $100 offered by the Galion City Council yesterday for the arrest of Frank Fisher will be paid to Officers Wurts and Nichols, who are deserving of high praise for the manner in which they hunted the villain down and captured him." [77]

The police committee of Galion City Council along with the City Solicitor were appointed to investigate the claims and disputes over the reward. The results from the investigation as reported follow:

"A Committee Appointed to Investigate the Matter – Some of the Evidence Adduced"

"The controversy over the reward offered by the city for the arrest of Frank Fisher, the ravisher, assumed such a complicated shape that the City Council deemed it necessary to have the matter thoroughly investigated before paying over the one hundred dollars, the amount of the reward offered. The labor of procuring evidence in the premises was turned over to the Committee on Police, of which

THE MOB LYNCHING OF FRANK FISHER

H.D. Lee is Chairman and Prosecutor DeGolly. The evidence thus far adduced is in the interest in the claims of Officers Nichols and Wurts. As it is a question giving rise to considerable comment and causing much feeling, we give below an outline of the evidence of the thus far examined.

The first affidavit taken was that of Cyrus H. George, of Independence, Richland County who deposed as follows: I am 32 years of age, and reside at Independence, Richland County, O., and am by occupation a laborer. I saw the arrest of Frank Fisher on the morning of the 30th day of April, A.D. 1882, at Fredericktown, Knox County, Ohio. The arrest occurred about 4:30 a.m. I was about 60 feet from the negro when I first saw him. Mr. T. J. Wurts had not yet approached near to him. I then saw Wurts go up to him and take hold of his left arm. W. H. W. Nichols then came up and searched the negro. The third man who walked up to the negro Frank Fisher was the Fredericktown Marshal, Braddock. I did not at any time see Fredericktown Marshal put his hand on the prisoner. Mr. Wurts and Mr. Nichols walked off with the prisoner and took charge of him. The Fredericktown Marshal told Messrs. Wurts and Nichols that they could put him in the lockup and could get him any time they wanted to. The reason they could not put the prisoner in the lockup is because they could not get the key into the lock. There were no other person present except, Wurts, Nichols, Braddock and myself. I was with the party half an hour after the arrest was made and never heard anyone claim that Braddock made the arrest. I saw Braddock first about 11:30 on the night previous to the arrest at the cigar store in Fredericktown; it was between 11 and 12 o'clock p.m. In my opinion he was under the influence of liquor.

At this point affiant was interrogated by Mr. H. D. Lee as follows:

Q. You can swear positively that Wurts made the arrest and Nichols then came up second and ordered the negro to hold up his hands and then searched him? A. Yes, I can, that is just the way it occurred.

Q. How far was Braddock off when you first saw Wurts and Nichols arrest the negro? A. Ten feet; he might have been farther.

Q. How did you happen to be in Fredericktown that night? A. I heard of the crime being committed and had seen a negro pass when I was working, and then started after him.

Q. How did you happen to come to Galion today? A. I received a note from my brother-in-law from Lexington to come to Lexington on the first train as they wished to see me. [The note is attached to this affidavit and made a part of the same, and marked "Exhibit A."] I went to Lexington, and then concluded I would go to Galion in person and make my statement.

Q. Did Mr. Wurts or Mr. Nichols have any talk with you in regard to the arrest and what you should say before or after you arrived at Galion? A. No, sir; they did not, neither did they send me any communication.

Q. In your opinion, from all the circumstances, has Mr. Braddock any right to the reward or any part of it? A. No, he has not; no more right than I would have, and I do not claim any part of it.

EXHIBIT A.

CY: - Come to Lexington on No. 8 tonight without fail. Hill and I sent in claim for part of the reward for catching the negro, and the Mayor of Galion wants a statement of the arrest, just how it happened, and we cannot give him a true statement without you being here. I think we will get part of the reward; so come without fail. Yours, A. W. H.

The following affidavit as to the veracity of Mr. George was presented:

State of Ohio. }

THE MOB LYNCHING OF FRANK FISHER

County of Crawford.}

Before me, a notary public in and for said County and State, personally came W. B. Hill who, being duly sworn, deposes and says that he is personally acquainted with Cyrus H. George and know him to be respectable and worthy of credit, and know that he was with the party referred to in his affidavit of said George at the time and place therein mentioned, as I started out with the party myself. The said Cyrus H. George is a man whose word can be relied upon.

Sworn to by the said W. B. Hill before me and him subscribed in my presence, this 9th day of May, A.D. 1882.

John D. DeGolly, Notary Public.

The affidavit of A. W. Berkett, who appeared before J. D. Hamilton, a Justice of the Peace of Richland County, recounts the manner in which he and his brother-in-law, C. H. George, proceeded in their search for the negro and concludes as follows: We then went back to Fredericktown and hunted up the Marshal, and was told by him that he had seen the negro not half an hour before on Main street. The Marshal acted strangely, and we dropped him and went and searched all of the negro houses in the town; this being about 11 o'clock p.m. The officers from Galion arrived just after we had made the above search and asked us whether we had seen anything of the negro. We told them we had not, but were satisfied we were very close to him, and he was certainly in or near town. They put up their team and we all started for the railroad. * * We (George and himself) came back to town about 2 o'clock a.m. and met Mr. Braddock, the Marshal intoxicated. We went to the hotel and lay down and rested until about 4 a.m. Then Hill, George and myself went to the planning mill and made a search of it. I told Mr. George to go up through the railroad cut and Hill and I would go around and come into the other end of it. We went to the other end of the cut and waited for Mr. George for a few minutes. Did not see him coming and went up town and met the Galion officers with the negro between them, and Mr. C. H. George was with them. We all then went to the hotel. I inquired of the negro if he had been in town that night, and he said no, but that he had slept in a barn north of town along the railroad track. We left the negro in the hands of the Galion officers and went home." [78]

"The reward over which the officers fought has not been paid. The Council will thoroughly investigate the matter, and pay the reward to the party to which it rightfully belongs." [79]

"The reward which the City Council offered for the arrest of Fisher has not yet been awarded. The police of Galion and the Marshall of Fredericktown both claim to have made the arrest. It will be decided by the Council and probably divided."[80]

The decision on the reward was not made by Galion City Council until two months after the bloody disagreement and the official investigation. On July 3, 1882 City Council passed a resolution allocating the reward money equally to Officers Wurts, Nichols and Marshall Braddock. [81]

A tragic ending for Marshal Braddock occurred eleven years later:

SUICIDED

Ex-Marshal Braddock of Fredericktown, Hangs Himself.

James D. Braddock, ex-marshal of Fredericktown, hung himself in his sister's barn last Friday morning.

He will be remembered as the marshal who was mixed up in the claim for the reward for the arrest of the negro rapist who was hung in this city on Sunday over eleven years ago, Braddock and Thos. J. Wurts (Wurtz) getting into a fight over the arrest and claim for reward, at the Central hotel. Wurts and Bill Nichols were really entitled to the reward, as subsequent events proved.

Braddock's mind gave way recently, and this induced his self-destruction. He was married last March to his second wife, Miss Laura Waddell, of Buckeye City, O., whom and his eleven-year-old daughter, he leaves to morn their loss. He was nearly 45 years old. [82]

The Aftermath and Investigation

"It is currently reported that the city officials are trying to make the Germans pay the cost of telegraphing in connection with the Fisher case. There is not a word of truth in the report. Mayor Underwood not having any money with him on the day of the outrage, and not wishing to lose any time, secured a small amount from a certain German citizen with the remark that he would see it was returned. This he did, and no citizen is called upon to pay out a cent for telegraphing or anything else in connection with this unfortunate affair." [83]

Almost immediately following Fisher's lynching the rumors regarding consequence for the numerous participants in the lynching where squelched.

"During the afternoon and evening the scene was visited by thousands of persons who feasted their prurient curiosity upon the picture of a human being hanging by the neck. There was seemingly but one sentiment. If any there were who deprecated the lynching, discretion suggested that they keep their thoughts to themselves. After the first strain of excitement had passed by the citizens viewed the matter in the light of a duty well performed, and discussed with each other the details with a nonchalance that was evidently not assumed." [84]

"There are not a dozen citizens of Galion who do not know just who did the horrid work, but we doubt much if any information can be obtained by the investigation which the grand jury will doubtless attempt to make."

Ultimately there was no investigation of any kind. All officials that might have conducted an investigation at either the federal, state, county or local level looked the other way.

THE MOB LYNCHING OF FRANK FISHER

"In the early evening Coroner Moffit of this city, was telegraphed for, but he declined to respond replying very laconically that if a mob of two thousand persons who bad hanged a man did not know how he came to his death, he did not think he could find out. None of the local justices of the peace cared to institute an investigation, and so the matter was allowed to go by default. Mayor Underwood ordered a guard to be kept during the night, and by the light of a bonfire a bevy of watchers kept vigil until day-light presenting a weird picture worthy the pencil of an artist." [85]

"By the better class of citizens, and looked upon with considerable regret, not because they think he did not deserve his fate, but because of the lawless and inhuman manner in which the whole affair was conducted." [86]

"A telegram had been sent to the Coroner soon after the lynching, but he did not come, and it was not until half past nine yesterday morning that the body was removed from the tree." [87]

"The lynching of Frank Fisher in broad daylight upon Sunday by unmasked men was one of the boldest affairs that has ever transpired in this County. While the affair is to be deeply regretted, yet the offense of the negro was such that he has not a word of sympathy from anyone who has heard the particulars of the crime which he has so dearly paid with his life. The Coroner of the County has been notified, and may yet tonight hold an inquest and render a verdict. There is some talk of having the leading lynchers indicted by the Grand Jury, but it would not be safe to attempt that at present." [88]

"There have been threats made today by a few lawyers to have the lynchers of Frank Fisher arrested, and in consequence mutterings and curses have been loud and deep from knots of people gathered upon the streets, and threats against anyone who dare make an arrest. The officials and officious will no doubt deem it best to let the lynching rest where it is for prudential reasons, although the terrible affair is to be deeply regretted and censured." [89]

"Later reports indicate a state of affairs at Galion that is amazing. Of course the best class of citizens deplore the outrage and feel that it is not only a deep disgrace but a serious damage to the city, and immediately following this open and undisguised defiance of the law, the citizens are made to realize that freedom of speech is suspended and that no one may even venture to regret it, under peril of personal injury, extending even the menace of death. Such are at least the reports from Gallon brought by eminently reliable citizens.

Thus not only was an infuriated mob enabled to openly defy the law, public opinion and every restraining influence, but having done so it has proceeded to place the whole city under a reign of terror, and no one, however great his respect for the law or however important his interest in the welfare of the city, may dare to speak his sentiments, lest his person be injured, his life placed in peril or his property destroyed." [90]

"There are but few people who condemn the deed, however lawless, and the general sentiment is that it was well done." [91]

"Corner Bauer refused to hold an inquest, and the body was turned over to the County Trustees for burial." [92]

"There seemed to be no one in particular who did the lynching. The feeling that summary Justice should be meted out to the rapist seemed to be felt by all classes of citizens. It was one of the most barefaced and systematic affairs of the kind that we have ever witnessed or seen chronicled. No attempt was made to mask or conceal identity, but everything was done openly and above board. After the last act of the tragedy was consummated the vast assemblage seemed to again breathe freely, and the universal opinion was expressed that the ravisher of Barbara Rettig had received his just dues." [93]

"It certainly was one of the boldest acts in the history of lynch law. None of the participators were masked and the victim was dragged from his cell in the broad light of a Sunday afternoon. There are not a dozen citizens of Galion who do not know just who did the horrid work, but we doubt much if any information can be obtained by the investigation which the grand jury will doubtless attempt to make.

In the early evening Coroner Moffit of this city, was telegraphed for, but he declined to respond replying very laconically that if a mob of two thousand persons who bad hanged a man did not know how he came to his death, he did not think he could find out. None of the local justices of the peace cared to institute an investigation, and so the matter was allowed to go by default." [94]

BILL BLOOMER LOCAL HISTORIAN:

"Souvenirs stripped the tree of its bark and the extra length of rope was cut into bits to be carried away and many feet of another rope was cut into small pieces and sold to the gullible to supply the demand.

The county coroner, for the fear of holding an inquest, failed to arrive, and Mayor Underwood ordered the body cut down at 10 a.m. The remains of the criminal were interred in Potters field of the Union Green cemetery quietly and without ceremony. A simple headboard bearing the letter M marked the grave.

The big town dailies carried front page stories and the people in all parts of the country brushed the dust off their maps to locate Galion, a snug little city that had become conspicuous overnight through mob violence-a mob's vengeance on the Sabbath Day, in the enlightened and presumed civilized, State of Ohio.

For years afterward, if a citizen ventured beyond the incorporated limits, he was sure to be questioned about the lynching and to explain just what part he personally played in the spectacle.

Sunday night and all day Monday, reporters representing big city papers swarmed into Galion. Medicos from the medical school came to claim the body. Crowds milled on the street corners, more strangers than townsmen.

Those who performed the leading roles became quite reticent and closemouthed as prosecution was threatened. For them, lapse of memory pervaded all those whom had taken even a minor part, but the few who favored the prosecution of the leaders soon became quiet as they were secretly warned that "there was still plenty of rope in Galion."

The lynching, having taken place in broad daylight without disguise of any kind and many of the leaders well known in the community, it was the unanimous opinion to drop the matter as quietly and quickly as possible, by calling it a closed incident and let the town resume the even tenor of its way." [95]

It should be noted the conflicting report of the name of the Coroner. The Galion Inquirer reported the coroner as Bauer and the Bucyrus Telegraph Forum reported the coroner as Moffit. Peter Bauer was a County Commissioner and previously ran for the office of coroner but was never elected as coroner.

The Opinions

Figure 23 - The Marion Star, May 1, 1882

"In the eyes of many was the appearance among the infuriated mob of so many women and children. The women seemed for the moment to have unsexed themselves, joining the throng, scaling fences, running across lots, and in every way acting as if they had lost their senses. Up to the very tree on which the doomed man was hung did they press, and seemed to gloat over the harrowing scene with a gusto that many men would not be guilty of. This was not confined to old and middle-aged women, but school girls and even children were among the number. It was a pitiable and lamentable sight, and one that reflects no credit upon those participating. Of course, to their honor be it said, there were a large portion of our lady citizens who shrank from this public exhibition of themselves, and deprecate in no unmeasured terms the unseemly conduct of their sisters. [96]

"During the past two weeks the people of this usually quiet and peaceful portion of the Buckeye Commonwealth have feasted upon horrors until their appetite has become more than satiated. The murder of Marshal Snodgrass was followed by a tragedy at Gallon in two acts, which exceeded in bloodthirsty inception and execution the killing of the Crestline official. There is no crime in the long list of felonies that so arouses public feeling and leads so quickly to the execution of summary punishment as that of rape. Murders may be committed in the heat of sudden passion, or even cool deliberation, and the sentiment of the public be slow to reach the point of unrestraint that leads to the inauguration of lynch law. For the crime of rape, however, there can be no excuse. It lacks every ingredient of motive except the satisfying of the most brutal passions. The safety of society demands protection against the conscienceless brutes who compel by force or threats innocent children to minister to their beastly lust. It is therefore not strange that the citizens of Galion and vicinity were aroused to frenzy by the crime of the negro Fisher but it is to be regretted that they allowed their feelings to lead them to the commission of an act that must remain ae an indelible stain upon the fame of our County for obedience to the behests of law." [97]

"Obviously the leaders in this sad affair must either be brought to justice or find safety in absence; and obviously, too, if this reign of terror is to continue the citizens must, as men, form a citizens' law and order league, and make common cause against those who have made common cause against the best interests of the city and County. Undoubtedly those most interested in the welfare and credit of Galion will know, at the proper time, how they can best vindicate the city and County from this deplorable catastrophe.

The Journal prefers to suspend all comment upon this deplorable affair for a week, while obviously, it cannot be defended, yet it has been stimulated by influences which are themselves indefensible, and which are even less excusable than the conduct of the leaders in this summary administration of punishment." [98]

"Hon. S. S. Bloom, of the Shelby News is giving an account of the lynching of Fisher in the city, takes occasion to make the following sensible remarks. "While it is true that such lawless proceedings are becoming far too common in Ohio for the reputation of the state, public opinion seems almost universally to endorse such acts of summary punishment. This simply proves that legislative action must be invoked to prevent the recurrence of them, and this must be in harmony with public sentiment, or else it will be of no avail to remedy the evil. If it be right to hang a person guilty of such a terrible outrage as this Fisher was guilty of – a rape of the most cruel, outrageous, horrible and fiendish we ever heard of – to terrible to even publish the facts, and we believe if any crime deserves the death penalty, such a one does, then we say it is right that the Legislature should say so at once, and thus legalize what the people will do without law. If it be right to hang such a villain instantly, this, too, can be done. Provision can be made to manacle, shackle and even tie down such a criminal so that escape is utterly impossible, and a trial immediately had and the demand for summary punishment be executed forthwith; but for a law and order loving State and people to sanction such proceedings until all law is laid aside, and mod law be inaugurated in place thereof, there ought to be but one view of the case. If even an extra session of the Legislature be necessary, better that it be at once called, and the demand of public sentiment crystalized into law, than that the authority of law should be constantly set aside and deeds done without law, that are beginning to spring up on every occasion." [99]

"During the afternoon and evening the scene was visited by thousands of persons who feasted their prurient curiosity upon the picture of a human being hanging by the neck. There was seemingly but one sentiment. If any there were who deprecated the lynching, discretion suggested that they keep their thoughts to themselves. After the first strain of excitement had passed by the citizens viewed the matter in the light of a duty well performed, and discussed with each other the details with a nonchalance that was evidently not assumed. It certainly was one of the boldest acts in the history of lynch law. None of the participators were masked and the victim was dragged from his cell in the broad light of a Sunday afternoon. There are not a dozen citizens of Galion who do not know just who did the horrid work, but we doubt much if any information can be obtained by the investigation which the grand jury will doubtless attempt to make.

In the early evening Coroner Moffit of this city, was telegraphed for, but he declined to respond replying very laconically that if a mob of two thousand persons who bad hanged a man did not know how he came to his death, he did not think he could find out. None of the local justices of the peace cared to institute an investigation, and so the matter was allowed to go by default. Mayor Underwood ordered a guard to be kept during the night, and by the light of a bonfire a bevy of watchers kept vigil until day-light presenting a weird picture worthy the pencil of an artist." [100]

"It is not strange that our nation is regarded by many Europeans as being but half civilized. The frequent execution of criminals, by a frenzied band of madmen, without regard to law, affords ground to believe, that, as a nation, we are not far removed from the customs of barbarians. Lynchings have become matters of almost daily occurrence, and instead of being regarded and treated as murders *which they are* the natural brute instinct of many men, gives them the color of justice, and the dastards who engage in them are called me of "courage" and "nerve" instead of receiving the punishment they so richly deserved.

On last Sunday, in an adjoining County, was enacted a scene which beggars description. A negro, who had committed a most heinous deed, was taken from proper authorities, and by a howling mob of men, whose actions were more like those of animals than of men, put to death. A defense of their action is impossible, for it was unwarranted. No palliation of the negro's crime can be made, he justly deserved the penalty he received, but that is not the point at issue. No man, however enormous his crime, should be punished unlawfully. No Man forfeits, his right to trial by jury, by the commission of any crime, and the man who attempts to punish crime *without* law, should be punished by law. In this ca se the offence committed was most horrible, but was it remedied by an act still more horrible? Will one crime expiate another? A violation of law in one point only insures a violation in another. Every act of mob violence serves to lower the standing of a people, and where mob law is most prevalent, there will be found the most lawless people. A criminal of the worse possible type has guaranteed to him the right of life, until he shall have been indicted, tried by jury, sentenced and executed according to law, and whoever takes, or assists to take his life otherwise, is a murderer and amenable to the same law the criminal may have violated. A summary dealing with men who take the law into their own hands in this manner, would prove most beneficial to community and perhaps put an end to a custom which is an outrage upon humanity." [101]

APPENDIX A

Ohio, Crawford County and Galion Population

	OHIO			CRAWFORD COUNTY			GALION		
	Total Population	Black Americans	% Black	Total Population	Black Americans	% Black	Total Population	Black Americans	% Black
1800	45,365	337	0.74%						
1810	230,760	1,899	0.82%						
1820	581,295	4,723	0.81%						
1830	937,903	9,574	1.02%	4,791	21	0.44%			
1840	1,519,467	17,345	1.14%	13,152	5	0.04%			
1850	1,980,329	25,279	1.28%	18,177	10	0.06%			
1860	2,339,511	36,673	1.57%	23,881	40	0.17%	1,966	2	0.10%
1870	2,665,260	63,213	2.37%	25,556	101	0.40%	3,523	22	0.62%
1880	3,198,062	80,142	2.51%	30,588	108	0.35%	5,635	31	0.55%
1890	3,672,616	87,113	2.37%	31,927	77	0.24%	6,326	23	0.36%
1900	4,157,545	96,901	2.33%	33,915	59	0.17%	7,282	19	0.26%
1910	4,767,121	111,452	2.34%	34,036	77	0.23%	7,214	14	0.19%
1920	5,759,394	185,187	3.22%	36,054	221	0.61%	7,374	5	0.07%
1930	6,646,697	309,304	4.65%	35,345	267	0.76%	7,674	1	0.01%
1940	6,907,612	339,461	4.91%	35,571	281	0.79%	8,685	4	0.05%
1950	7,946,627	513,072	6.46%	38,738	245	0.63%	9,592	3	0.03%

APPENDIX B

The Participants

The following is a brief history of the people directly involved and those that played other various roles in Galion at the time of the lynching of Frank Fisher:

Frank Fisher (*alleged perpetrator*) was NOT present in the 1880 census for Galion and Crawford County. There is a Frank Fisher, black, age 29 present in the 1880 census of Columbus, Franklin County, Ohio. This is most likely the Frank Fisher of this story. The census indicates Frank Fisher was born in Kentucky as was his mother and father. The 1880 census indicates he resided at the corner of Fair Alley and South Street and was working in a livery stable. After an extensive search of records, it appears according to the 1880 census, Fisher's mother was living in Louisville, Ky. According to that record Mary Fisher was born abt. 1824, was a widow and working as a servant. She lived in what appears to be servants housing at 509 Breckinridge Street. There is an extensive list of servants and family members all living under the same address as the Augustus Jacob family, who was a foreman at the Turner, Day & Woolworth Manufacturing Company.

Barbara Rettig, (*alleged victim*) born on April 14, 1869, in Lautern, Hesse, Germany, her father, Peter, was 26, and her mother, Anna, was 25. Barbara arrived in America on May 24, 1881 from Germany with her parents and six other siblings. She married George Washington Nungesser on November 22, 1887. They had four children during their marriage. She died on January 31, 1932, at the age of 62 and was buried in Crestline, Ohio.

Peter Rettig, (*father of alleged victim*) born September 26, 1842, died November 21, 1923, arrived in America on May 24 1881 from Germany along with his wife Anna Eva Boehm (married November 26, 1865) and seven children including Barbara. His occupation was listed as "tailor". Lived on farm in Polk Township in 1890 census with wife Eva and five children (4 born in Ohio). In 1910 census Peter is listed as head of household and widowed. Peter is buried in Fairview Cemetery.

Anna Eva (Boehm) Rettig, (*mother of alleged victim*) was born on December 18, 1843, in Germany, the daughter of Elisabetha and Johann. She married Peter Rettig on November 26, 1865. They had 13 children in 20 years.

She died on September 5, 1904, in Galion, Ohio, at the age of 60, and was buried there.

Jerimiah (Jerry) Myers, (*reported to be employer of Frank Fisher*) was born on November 24, 1820, in Bellville, Ohio, his father, Jacob, was 38 and his mother, Sarah, was 32. He married Sarah Jane Long on March 18, 1841. They had ten children in 20 years. He died on January 21, 1895, in Galion, Ohio, at the age of 74, and was buried there. Republican but also ran as an Independent (where he lost) after losing a republican endorsement.

Abraham Underwood (*Democrat, Mayor and Justice of the Peace for Polk Township*), Born December 3, 1814 in Wayne County, Ohio, his father, Elihu, was 20 and his mother, Margaret, was 18. His parents were born in Pennsylvania. In 1850 census his occupation was listed as "tailor". In 1860 census was 46 years old and married to Sarah Madlum, 40 years old (married July 28, 1842 in Richland County, Ohio). His occupation was "attorney". In 1870 census he was listed separately from Sarah and their children. His occupation was "Attorney at Law". In 1880 census was 65 years old and married to Agnes Kear, 37 years old (married August 30, 1876 in Wyandot, Ohio). His occupation was listed as "justice of the peace". He died June 20, 1898 and was buried at Fairview Cemetery.

Matthias Wisler (*Democrat, Council President and First Ward Councilmember*) Wisler was born on December 29, 1826, in Staufen, Baden-Württemberg, Germany, his father, Joseph, was 47 and his mother, Katharina, was 21. He married Lusia Faller on January 15, 1854 in Dayton, Ohio. They had 11 children in 23 years. He died on March 20, 1894, in Galion, Ohio, at the age of 67, and was buried at Mt. Calvary cemetery. Wisler was a well-known east end grocer. He was elected councilman for three terms before the city was divided into wards, and as president for four years. "He was many times appointed to different offices and positions of trust, and at all times was an honored and honest citizen."

Charles Jefferson Crissinger (*Democrat, First Ward Councilmember*) When Charles Crissinger was born on August 6, 1845, in Ohio, his father, Jacob, was 33 and his mother, Elizabeth Coblen, was 28. He married Sevilla Noblet on December 21, 1871. They had one child during their marriage. He died on January 31, 1926, at the age of 80, and was buried in Galion, Ohio. Crissinger controlled a large amount of the real estate and insurance business at Gallon. Until he was sixteen years of age, when he started out to take care of himself, Charles J. Crissinger attended school and gave his father assistance. He continued to work at farming until he was twenty-three years old and then learned the carpenter trade, which he followed until 1887, when he embarked in the grocery business and continued until 1901. In that year he disposed of his grocery interests and went into the real estate and insurance business and has been very successful.

William I. Goshorn (*Democrat, Second Ward Councilmember and Police Committee*) When William Isaac Goshorn was born on March 11, 1838, in Tell, Pennsylvania, his father, Samuel, was 29 and his mother, Eleanor, was 23. He married Ellen E. Strong on May 16, 1877, in Homer, Michigan. They had two children during their marriage. He died on August 23, 1893, in Galion, Ohio, at the age of 55, and was buried there.

Henry David Lee (*Republican, Second Ward Councilmember and Police Committee*) was born in Vermont, parents from Canada and born in Ireland. H.D. was an oil merchant was 31 years old in 1880 census. Married Emma L. Colburn on August 2, 1869 in Crawford County. In 1870 was living with his wife's parents.

He moved to Galion in 1867 where he worked as a hotel clerk and parlayed early business success selling circular knitting machines into the purchase of Central Oil Co. of Galion. Later the Standard Oil Company purchased the refinery and he remained for a time as President. He then retired, having accumulated a fortune in his thirties.

That early success in the oil industry coupled with advice from his doctor (he was tubercular) to move to a drier climate, led Lee to move to Salina, Kansas in 1889 and set up The H.D. Lee Mercantile Co., soon becoming the major food distributor between Kansas City and Denver.

Later the product range was expanded to include Sales of notions, furnishings, stationery and school supplies. In 1912, The H.D. Lee Mercantile Co. opened its first garment factory making work wear and hence the Lee Jeans brand was born.

Lee established brand loyalty early with current and aspiring cowboys and rodeo champions, in part by improving fabric, fit and finishes to meet their specific needs. Copper rivets were replaced with "scratch-proof" stitching to reinforce back pockets, protecting saddles—the cowboy's most valued possession. Lee Cowboy Pants later became known as Lee Riders.

Samuel Gochenour (*Democrat, Third Ward Councilmember*) Samuel Gochenour was born in October 1830 in Pennsylvania. He married Louisa Hipsher on May 21, 1859, in Caledonia, Ohio. They had four children in 13 years. He died on February 27, 1911, in Galion, Ohio, having lived a long life of 80 years. Gochenour was a conductor on the B. & I. railroad for several years and later was in the business conducting a grocery.

Anthony Long (*Democrat, Third Ward Councilmember and Police Committee*) Anthony Long was born in 1824 in Baden-Württemberg, Germany. He married Mary Ann "Johanna" Reister on November 2, 1846, in Crawford, Ohio. They had seven children in 15 years. He died on July 1, 1888, in Galion, Ohio, at the age of 64, and was buried there.

David Mackey (*Republican, Fourth Ward Councilmember*) When David Leonard Mackey was born on April 3, 1835, in Pennsylvania, his father, William, was 32 and his mother, Rossana, was 20. He had one son from one relationship. He then married Sarah Louisa Traul and they had two children together. He died on December 11, 1906, in Galion, Ohio, at the age of 71, and was buried there. Mackey early in his work career was a carpenter building houses and later in life a merchant salesman.

Patrick M. Daily (*Republican, Fourth Ward Councilmember*) Patrick McKelvey Daily was born on May 27, 1825, in Holmes, Ohio. He married Lacy Ann Davis on July 10, 1861. They had one child during their marriage. He died on November 19, 1910, in Galion, Ohio, having lived a long life of 85 years, and was buried in Fairview Cemetery. Daily worked in farming and as a grocer.

John D. De Golley (*Democrat, City Prosecutor*) was born in May 1855 in Maryland, the son of Susan and Abraham. He was married three times and had two sons. He died on March 6, 1927, in Ohio at the age of 71, and was buried in Galion, Ohio.

William Blacksten, (*Democrat, Marshal*), born March 15, 1837 in Ohio, died January 20, 1914 in Mansfield, Ohio in Ohio (both parents from Pennsylvania), lived in North Robinson at the 1880 census, married to Mary Roma Teeple (October 2, 1864 in Morrow County, Ohio), 1870 census was a marble cutter, 1910 census lived with 2 sisters on N Columbus Street in Galion.

William H. W. Nichols (*Officer*) was born on March 25, 1834, in Pottstown, Pennsylvania, his father, Matthias, was 39 and his mother, Sarah, was 36. He married Mary Louise Hiltabidle and they had 11 children together. He also had two sons and three daughters from another relationship. He died on October 25, 1921, in Galion, Ohio, at the age of 87, and was buried in Polk, Ohio.

Herman Zeller (*Chief of Fire Department*) When Herman Zeller was born on September 17, 1843, in Baden-Württemberg, Germany, his father, John, was 45 and his mother, Josepha, was 29. He married Mary Elizabeth Fehr and they had four children together. He also had two sons and one daughter from another relationship. He died on September 4, 1913, in Morrow, Ohio, at the age of 69, and was buried in Galion, Ohio.

At a young age Zeller went to California and for 12 years and worked in the gold fields. He then returned to Galion and engaged in the meat business. For a long period of years he conducted a meat market on East Main Street, in the Joe Motsch room, with Mr. Motsch as partner. Later he conducted a shop on the east side, retiring from business in 1892, to become a policeman, serving faithfully in that capacity until 1908 when his retirement was forced because of ill health.

Zeller was a public spirited citizen. For many years during the regime of the volunteer fire department and some years after the paid fire department was organized, he was chief of the fire department of the city. He was a member of the old Niagara fire company and shared the honors achieved by that remarkable organization of fire fighters.

John C. Beltz (*Democrat, Polk township trustee and farmer*) one of the old and well known residents of Crawford County, lived on his farm of 84 acres, in Polk township, three miles west of Galion.

Beltz came to this County with his parents when a boy of six years. He was born in Center County. Pa., April 19, 1823. He assisted his father on the farm and received his schooling in the old log school house which stood on his father's farm, attending school when the weather was too bad to work. He has lived on the farm ever since he came to the County, a period of 83 years. On April 19, 1845, his 22nd birthday, he married Miss Nancy Reed, who died Dec. 26, 1899 and was buried at Gallon. She was a daughter of David and Elizabeth (Pletcher) Reed.

Mr. Beltz is a Democrat in politics and was trustee of Polk Township several terms. He belonged to the English Lutheran church

W. M. Zimmerman (*Democrat, Polk Township Trustee*) When William Zimmerman was born on April 22, 1843, in Whetstone, Ohio, his father, Daniel, was 29 and his mother, Charlotte, was 32. He married Sarah Ann Christman on March 18, 1866. They had one child during their marriage. He died on September 17, 1922, at the age of 79, and was buried in Fairview Cemetery.

Jacob Ernst (*Democrat, Polk Township Trustee*) Jacob Ernst was born on June 22, 1828, in Bavaria, Germany. He married Elizabeth Reber on April 23, 1857, in Ashland, Ohio. They had six children in 17 years. He died on August 24, 1882, in Crawford, Ohio, at the age of 54, and was buried in Mount Calvary Cemetery. Ernst was a boot and shoemaker and proprietor of the Ernst Shoe Store.

Adam (Ted) Werts (*Democrat, Polk Township Constable*), was born in September 1830 in Ohio, his father, David, was 21 and his mother, Anna, was 24. He married Mary L Miller on April 15, 1850. He died on August 4, 1905, in Crawford, Ohio, at the age of 74. The 1850 census list his employment as farmer. The 1870 census indicates Adam worked as a clerk in a saloon. The 1880 and 1900 census indicates he worked as a constable.

Thomas. J. Wurtz (*Democrat, Polk Township Constable*) T J Wurts was born on April 4, 1846, in Wayne, Ohio. He married Hattie Felix on November 1, 1868, in his hometown. They had six children in 20 years. He died suddenly on December 17, 1893, in Galion, Ohio, at the age of 47, and was buried in Fairview Cemetery. He was a plasterer and painter by trade.

George M. Ziegler (*Lawyer and Former Prosecutor*), address 16 North Union Street, 1880 census was 30 years old, occupation "lawyer", marital status "single". 1870 census was living at home in Liberty Township, Crawford County, Ohio as a "student". His father George L. Ziegler was a "physician". George L. Ziegler's parents were born in Germany. 1860 census was living at home in Liberty Township, Crawford County, Ohio. 1850 census was living at home and was listed as 4 years old. (State Representative from 1883-1885) Prosecuting Attorney 1878

Philip J Moffit (*Democrat, Coroner*) born in June, 1823 in Huron County, Ohio. Was a farmer and auctioneer from Chatfield Township in Crawford

County? He Died May 29, 1882. Elected corner in 1870, 1872, 1874 and 1881.

Peter Bauer (*Democrat, County Commissioner*) For seven years served as a County commissioner of Crawford County, O. and a farmer of Jackson Township. He was born in Vernon Township, Crawford County, Feb. 23, 1837, and is a son of John Philip and A. Catherine (Fike) Bauer.

Peter Bauer grew up on his father's farm in Vernon Township. He was a lifelong Democrat, and frequently had been called to public office. In 1873 he was elected a County commissioner and served continuously until 1880. Then he retired from this office. Bauer was married to Miss Elizabeth Cook, who was born in Richland County, Ohio, Aug. 4, 1842, and died June 6, 1914.

Marshall James D. Braddock (*Marshal, Fredericktown, Ohio*) When James D. Braddock was born on December 2, 1848, in Fredericktown, Ohio, his father, Joshua, was 30 and his mother, Margaret, was 29. In the 1870 census his occupation was listed as "farm laborer" and in the 1980 census his occupation was listed as "butcher". He married Nora A. Phillips on December 22, 1870, they had one daughter together. Nora died on March 24, 1891, in her hometown at the age of 39, and was buried in Fredericktown, Ohio. He then married Laura A Waddell on March 29, 1893. James D. Braddock committed suicide on June 30, 1893 in his hometown at the age of 44, and was buried there.

Cyrus H. George (*Affidavit Provider*) When Cyrus H. George was born on August 6, 1849, in Lexington, Ohio, his father, William, was 23 and his mother, Mary, was 23. He married Priscilla Winbigler and they had three children together. He also had one son with Ethel Lake. He died on August 14, 1933, in his hometown at the age of 84, and was buried there.

Wilson B. Hill (*Affidavit Provider*) W. B. Hill was born in 1842 in Holmes, Ohio, the son of Margaret and Abraham. He married Anna Snyder on May 14, 1868, in Morrow, Ohio. They had six children in 12 years. He died on May 11, 1891, in Richland, Ohio, at the age of 49, and was buried in Lexington, Ohio.

William C. Craven, M.D. (*Cleveland Doctor*) was born in May 1848 in Ohio. He married Sabra Celinda Giddings on October 28, 1874, in Cuyahoga, Ohio. They had three children in 17 years. He died on November 14, 1924, in Los Angeles, California, at the age of 76, and was buried in Glendale, California.

Phillip Herbold (*Undertaker and Cabinet Maker*), address 19 Main Street, Phillip and his son Phillip Jr. were cabinet makers. Phillip was born in Germany on February 27, 1820. He was married to Friedericka Feldmann on August 10, 1848. His son Phillip Jr. was born in Ohio around 1860. 1870 census list Phillip as "cabinet maker and undertaker". Died January 18, 1911.

John Keil (*County Sheriff*) When John Keil was born on February 1, 1836, in Darmstadt, Hesse, Germany, his father, Johann, was 32 and his mother, Eva, was 23. Prior to immigrating to the United States in 1854 he learned the blacksmith trade. After being employed at his trade for Phillip Osman for a year and a half, formed a partnership with Nicholas Bormuth, he building a blacksmith. During the civil war he gave his entire attention to dealing in horses for cavalry service. In the year 1865 he started into the grocery business with John Kaler and C G Malic.

In the years 1881 and 1883 he was elected sheriff of Crawford County and again in the years 1893 and 1895. He was the only man who after being sheriff for four years was again elected to the position for four years more. Mr. Keil also served the city of Bucyrus as a member of the board of Public Service from the year 1905 until 1907 after which time he retired from active duties.

He married Wilhelmina Hocker on April 3, 1856. They had 12 children in 24 years. He died on February 8, 1913, in Bucyrus, Ohio, and was buried there.

Anson Wickham (*Democrat, County Prosecutor*) attorney at law at Bucyrus, Ohio, and president of the Bar Association of Crawford County, has been prominent in his profession for many years, during the larger number of which he has been a resident of Bucyrus.

He was born on a farm in Crawford County in June, 1849, and grew to manhood thereon. He is a son of Willard and Phoebe (Pennington) Wickham, the father being a native of New York and of English ancestry. The mother was from Virginia, being of Irish and German ancestry. They had a family of seven children.

In May, 1893, Mr. Wickham was married to Catharine Shellhase who was born in Prussia. Her parents immigrated to this country when Catharine was of tender years and settled in Jefferson Township, Crawford County, where she resided until the decease of her parents which occurred in 1886-7, after which she moved to the city of Bucyrus. For the past few years Mr. and Mrs. Wickham have been practically living under the eaves of the courthouse

Richard Wallace Cahill (*Democrat, delegate to 1850 Ohio Constitutional Convention representing Crawford County*) When Richard Wallace Cahill was born on March 6, 1803, in Westmoreland County, Pennsylvania, his father, Abraham, was 38 and his mother, Agnes, was 36. In 1818 he came with his parents to Wayne County, Ohio, and in June 1827, came to Bucyrus, Ohio where until 1833, he clerked in a store, at that date he removed to Vernon Township, where he lived for over a half century. At that time Vernon was part of Richland County. In 1841 he was elected to represent Richland County in the State Legislature. He was reelected in 1842 and 1843.In February 1845 Wayne County was created, and by the change Vernon township was made a part of Crawford County. Cahill represented Crawford County at the Ohio Constitutional Convention of 1850.

He married Eliza Elizabeth Cummins and they had four children together. He also had one son from another relationship. He then married Catharine Richards and they had 13 children together. He died on October 2, 1886, in Crawford, Ohio, having lived a long life of 83 years, and was buried in Tiro, Ohio.

APPENDIX C

The Places

City Hall and Opera House

In 1873 it was agreed by the authorities of Polk Township and those of the corporation of Galion to erect a building for a court room and other public offices. After much discussion in regard to location, lot 48 of Michael and Jacob Ruhl's second Addition to Galion was selected. The building was to be 66 x 75 feet in ground dimensions, three stories in height, and built of brick and stone. In 1875 the contract was awarded to George Wimmie and in the following year the building was completed. The lower story contained one storeroom, two election rooms (one for the city and one for township), one room for Star steamer and hose-cart and one jail room. The second story had six rooms, among them being the mayor's and justice's court room and a room to be used temporarily as an infirmary. In the third story was the opera hall, with stage and other accessories.

Fire Department Headquarters and Prison

The first fire department headquarters and jail was completed in 1870 and located at 114 Atwood Street between South Market Street and Union Street. There were two jail cells constructed on the second floor. It remained the headquarters for the fire department until 1886. This jail was reported to be the jail Frank Fisher was taken to after his arrest.

Central Hotel

The Central Hotel (located at the city square) was built in 1852 by Joel and David Riblet and was occupied as a dry goods store and dwelling. One year later Brown and McMillan opened a hotel in it and called it the Western. In 1881 there were 86 sleeping rooms, three sample rooms and a dining room with a capacity of 66 seats. The Central was the location of the fight between Marshal Braddock of Fredericktown and Officers Nichols and Wurts.

Union Green Cemetery

The Union Green cemetery was located on land donated by Jacob Ruhl. Just north of this cemetery is the Catholic cemetery. After the Lutheran church was built near the cemetery in 1840 that church added more land, and in 1861 a final addition was made to it on the south side by Daniel Riblet. This addition brought the cemetery ground up to Church Street and made it a block in size, about five acres. The rapid growth of the town after 1850 led to several propositions for a new and larger cemetery, but it was not until thirty years later that definite action was taken and the site of the present Fairview Cemetery secured, a tract of 80 acres near the northeastern part of the city. Frank Fisher was buried in Potters field in Union Green Cemetery. The last burial was made in Union Green Cemetery in 1910.

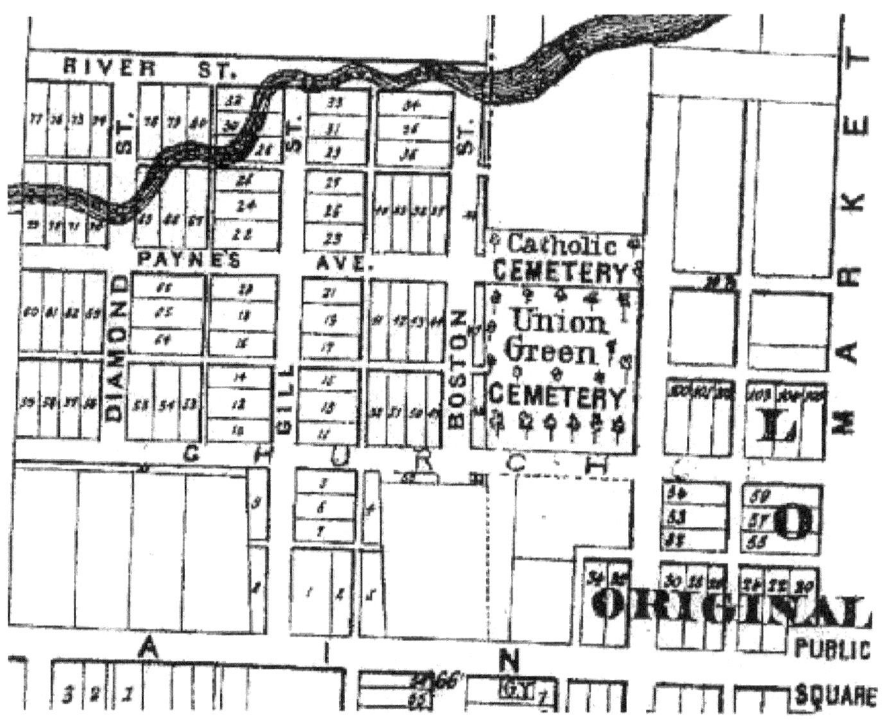

Fairview Cemetery

Fairview Cemetery records begin in January, 1883, when the first burial took place. Transfer of disinterments from Union Green Cemetery began soon thereafter.

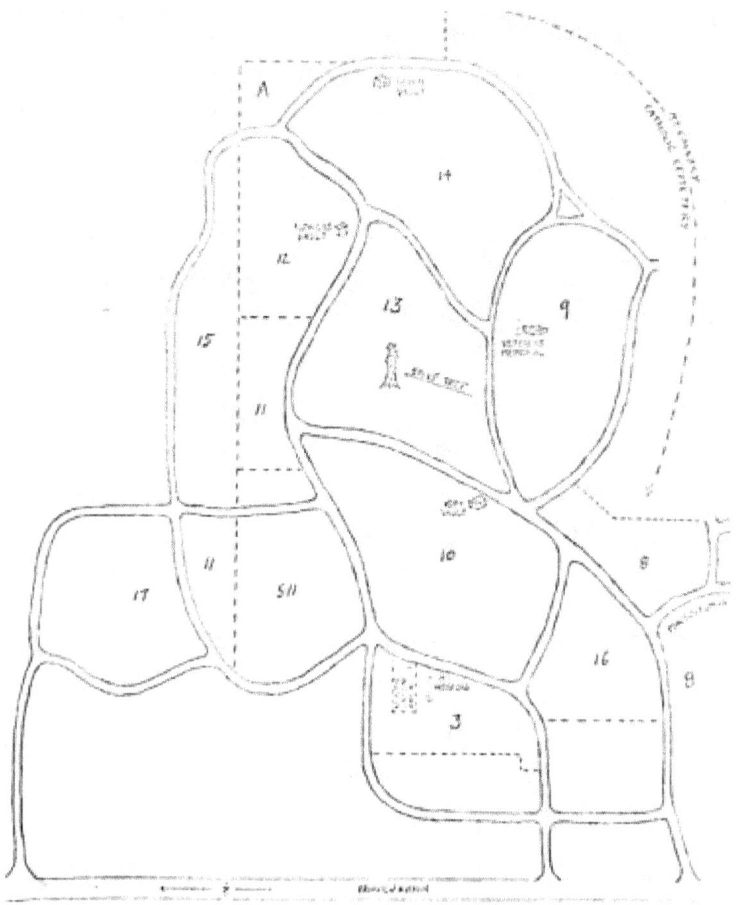

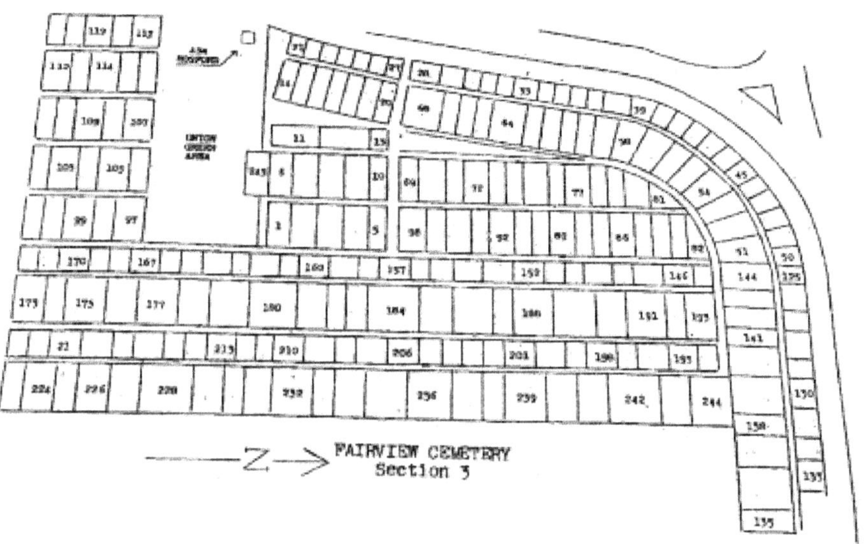

FAIRVIEW CEMETERY
Section 3

APPENDIX D
LEAVE PROBLEM TO THE SOUTH.
That is Arkansas Bishop's Advice on the Race Question.
Says Lynching Seems Only Punishment for Certain Crimes.
Cleveland Plain Dealer, September 18, 1903.

"Bishop William M. Brown of Arkansas was at the Hollenden yesterday en route from his summer home at Galion, O., to Washington D. C., where he will attend the conventions of the American house of the bishops of Episcopal churches and the missionary council of the Episcopal Church. Bishop Brown is an Ohio man, having formerly been archdeacon of the northern Ohio diocese. He has been bishop of Arkansas for five years and has made particular study of the negro question which has especially agitated that state.

"I am of the conviction," said the bishop, "that it would be well to leave the solution of this potent problem largely to the people of the south. It is one which concerns them most, and being on the ground, so to speak, they are better able to judge what would be the best solution of the problem. The people of Arkansas are, as a whole, an educated and especially broad minded people and are fully able to cope with the question in their state. I am the first northern man assigned to a southern bishopric and when I went south I had, of course, about the same idea of this question as is largely prevalent in the north."

"I consider the enfranchisement of the negro has been a serious mistake. Uneducated as he is, he is but a tool and as was in the hands of the politicians. Very few of them have any convictions and their votes are cast for the man who has paid the highest price for it. While in some localities in Arkansas the negro's outnumbers the white population, the whites have managed by hook or crook to keep the control of affairs in their hands, therefore a negro is never elected to office. The resulting evil from enfranchisement of the negro is, however, that a candidate who has no attributes whatever to recommend his election to office, is often able by a liberal supply of currency to purchase the negro vote and thus secure election."

Asked his opinion on the lynching problem, Bishop Brown replied. "While I do not justify lynching, I know of no other punishment which is adequate to suppress the crime for which lynching is usually resorted to. Imprisonment has no effect upon the southern negro. His return from serving a penitentiary sentence is usually the occasion for a glorification in the community where he resides, and he is treated a hero. In many cases it would be impossible through lack of prosecution, prompted by delicacy, to secure a conviction and punishment by law."

FIGURES

BIBLIOGRAPHY

Berwanger, Eugene H. 1971. *The Frontier Against Slavery.* Urbana, Illinois: University of Illinois Press.

Gerber, David A. 1976. "Black Ohio and the Color Line, 1860-1915." 23-24.

Gray, Wood. 1942. *The Hidden Civil War.* New York: The Viking Press.

Klement, Frank L. 1960. *The Copperheads in the Middle West.* Chicago, Illinois: The University of Chicago Press.

Litwach, Lein F. 1961. *North of Slavery.* Chicago, Illinois: The University of Chicago Press.

Middleton, Stephen. 2005. *The Black Laws: Race and the Legal Process in Early Ohio.* Athens, Ohio: Ohio University Press.

Milton, George Fort. n.d. *Abraham Lincoln and The Fifth Column.*

Scarselli, Steven H. Steinglass & Gino J. 2004. "The Ohio Constitution A Reference Guide."

Tarr, G. Alan. n.d. "The Ohio Constitution of 1802: An Introduction."

Walker, David Myers and Elise Meyers. 2019. *Lynching and Mob Violence in Ohio, 1772-1938.* First. Jefferson, North Carolina: McFarland & Company, Inc.

Weber, Jennifer L. 2010. "Lincoln's Critics: The Copperheads."

Yager, Brian. 2016. "Northwest Ohio Political Sentiment During The Civil War."

ENDNOTES

[1] Stephen Middleton, *The Black Laws,* (Ohio University Press, 2005)

[2] Paul Finkelman, *The Strange Career of Race Discrimination in Antebellum Ohio,* (2004)

[3] David A. Gerber, *Black Ohio and The Color Line,* 1860-1915, at 23-24 (1976)

[4] John E. Hopely, *History of Crawford County and Representative Citizens* (Richard-Arnold Publishing, 1912), 133

[5] Hopley, *History of Crawford County,* 131-132

[6] Hopley, *History of Crawford County,* 132

[7] Hopley, *History of Crawford County,* 132-133

[8] "Vengeance Is Mine", *Bucyrus Telegraph Forum,* May 5, 1882.

[9] "Vengeance Is Mine", *Bucyrus Telegraph Forum.*

[10] "Brutal Outrage", *Marion Star,* April 29, 1882.

[11] "Pursuing A Ravisher", *Cincinnati Enquirer,* April 29, 1882.

[12] "Mob Law", *Cincinnati Enquirer,* May 1, 1882.

[13] "Lynched" *Galion Inquirer,* May 4, 1882.

[14] "Mob Law In Crawford County", *Bucyrus Journal,* May 5, 1882.

[15] "Dragged To Death", *Cleveland Plain Dealer,* May 1, 1882.

[16] "A Horrible Case of Outrage on a Little Girl", *Ohio State Journal,* April 28, 1882

[17] "German Girl Outraged by a "colored" Brute", *Columbus Dispatch,* April 29, 1882

[18] "Frank Fisher Lynched", *Columbus Dispatch,* May 1, 1882

[19] "Horrible Treatment of a Young Girl by a Negro", *Cleveland Leader,* April 29, 1882

[20] "Lynched!", *Cleveland Leader,* May 1, 1882

[21] Mansfield, *The Olentangy Legacy Book Two,* Xlibris, 38

[22] "Lynched", *Galion Inquirer.*

[23] "Lynched", *Galion Inquirer.*

[24] City of Galion, Meeting Minutes, April 29, 1882.

[25] "Pursuing a Ravisher", *Cincinnati Enquirer.*

[26] "Lynched", *Galion Inquirer.*

[27] "Brutal Outrage", *Marion Star*

[28] "Mob Law In Crawford County", *Bucyrus Journal.*

[29] "Searching for a Fiend", *St. Louis Dispatch,* April 28, 1882.

[30] "Vengeance Is Mine", *Bucyrus Telegraph Forum*

[31] "Evidently a Mistake in the Person", *Ohio State Journal*, April 29, 1882

[32] "Looking for a Ravisher", *Cincinnati Enquirer*, April 30, 1882.

[33] "Fiendish Fisher", *Ohio State Journal*, April 30, 1882.

[34] Mansfield, *The Olentangy Legacy Book Two*, Xlibris, 39-40

[35] "Vengeance is Mine", *Bucyrus Telegraph Forum*.

[36] "Lynched", *Cleveland Leader*.

[37] "Vengeance Is Mine", *Bucyrus Telegraph Forum*.

[38] "Lynched", *Galion, Inquirer*.

[39] Mansfield, *The Olentangy Legacy*, 40

[40] "Lynched", *Cleveland Leader*.

[41] "The Fiend Caught – Probably the Right Man", *Ohio State Journal*, April 30, 1882.

[42] "Mob Law In Crawford County", Bucyrus Journal.

[43] "Concerning the Lynching of Fisher", *Cincinnati Enquirer*, May 2, 1882.

[44] "Mob Law", *Cincinnati Enquirer*.

[45] "Vengeance Is Mine", *Bucyrus Telegraph Forum*.

[46] "Lynched", *Cleveland Leader*.

[47] Mansfield, *The Olentangy Legacy*, 42

[48] "Lynched", *Cleveland Leader*.

[49] "Fisher Lynched at Galion Yesterday by a Mob", *Cleveland Leader*, April 30, 1882.

[50] "Latest Particulars of the Lynching", *Ohio State Journal*, April, 30, 1882.

[51] "Lynched", *Marion Star*, May 1, 1883.

[52] "Frank Fisher Lynched", *Columbus Dispatch*.

[53] "Lynched", *Cleveland Leader*.

[54] "Mob Law", *Cincinnati Enquirer*.

[55] "Dragged To Death", *Cleveland Plain Dealer*.

[56] "Mob Law In Crawford County", *Bucyrus Journal*.

[57] "Vengeance Is Mine", *Bucyrus Telegraph Forum*.

[58] "Lynched", *Galion Inquirer*.

[59] "Concerning the Lynching of Fisher", *Cincinnati Enquirer*.

[60] Mansfield, *The Olentangy Legacy*, 41

[61] "Vengeance Is Mine", *Bucyrus Telegraph Forum*.

[62] "Lynched", *Galion Inquirer*.

[63] "Mob Law In Crawford County", *Bucyrus Journal*.

[64] "Frank Fisher's Funeral", *Cleveland Plain Dealer*, May 3, 1882.

[65] "Burial of Fisher", *The Rapist*, Cincinnati Enquirer, May 3, 1882.

[66] "Lynched", *Galion Inquirer*.

[67] "Lynched", *Galion Inquirer*.

[68] "Vengeance Is Mine", *Bucyrus Telegraph Forum*.

[69] "Lynched", *Galion Inquirer*.

[70] "Vengeance Is Mine", *Bucyrus Telegraph Forum*.

[71] "The Fisher Reward – An Idle Rumor Refuted", *Galion Inquirer*, May 11, 1882.

[72] "Vengeance Is Mine", *Bucyrus Telegraph Forum*.

[73] "Lynched", *Galion Inquirer*.

[74] "Concerning the Lynching of Fisher", *Cincinnati Enquirer*.

[75] "Mob Law In Crawford County", *Bucyrus Journal*.

[76] "Burial of Fisher - The Rapist", *Cincinnati Enquirer*.

[77] "Mob Law", *Cincinnati Enquirer*.

[78] "The Fisher Reward", *Galion Inquirer*, May 11, 1882.

[79] "Lynched", *Galion Inquirer*.

[80] "Fisher Fiend Burial", *Columbus Dispatch*, May 2, 1882.

[81] City of Galion, "Meeting Minutes, July 3, 1882.

[82] "Suicided", *Galion Inquirer*, July 14, 1893

[83] "Lynched", *Galion Inquirer*.

[84] "Vengeance Is Mine", *Bucyrus Telegraph Forum*.

[85] "Vengeance Is Mine", *Bucyrus Telegraph Forum*.

[86] "Lynched", *Cleveland Leader*.

[87] "Fisher Fiend Burial", *Columbus Dispatch*.

[88] "Mob Law", *Cincinnati Enquirer*.

[89] "Concerning the Lynching of Fisher", *Cincinnati Enquirer*.

[90] "Mob Law In Crawford County", Bucyrus Journal.

[91] "Dragged To Death", *Cleveland Plain Dealer*.

[92] "Lynched", *Galion Inquirer*.

[93] "Lynched", *Galion Inquirer*.

[94] "Vengeance Is Mine", *Bucyrus Telegraph Forum*.

[95] Mansfield, *The Olentangy Legacy*, 44-45

[96] "Lynched", *Galion Inquirer*.

[97] "Vengeance Is Mine", *Bucyrus Telegraph Forum*.

[98] "Mob Law In Crawford County", *Bucyrus Journal*.

[99] "Mob Law", *Galion Inquirer*, May 11, 1882.

[100] "Vengeance Is Mine", *Bucyrus Telegraph Forum*.

[101] "Mob Lawlessness", *Ohio Liberal*, May 3, 1882.

Don't miss out!

Visit the website below and you can sign up to receive emails whenever Mike Robinette publishes a new book. There's no charge and no obligation.

https://books2read.com/r/B-A-AKOP-CSLWB

BOOKS 2 READ

Connecting independent readers to independent writers.

About the Author

Mike Robinette

An avid american history buff and ameteur researcher, *The MOB Lynching of Frank Fisher* is Mike's first book.